*"Burnt are our homes, exiled our chiefs
Scattered the loyal men"*

These lines from the Skye Boat Song describe the aftermath of the Battle of Culloden – where the Scottish Highlanders fighting for the Stuart cause were mercilessly butchered and their women and children left to die. But the verse conceals the stirring story of courage and sacrifice by clansmen who fought gallantly against tremendous odds for a cause that is forever tied up with the magic of the name of "Bonnie Prince Charlie."

The story of the Jacobite rebellions began with James II, grandfather of the Prince, who was forced from his throne by William of Orange in the "Glorious Revolution" of 1688. For more than fifty years, the exiled Stuarts and their Jacobite followers fought to regain the throne. Using a wide selection of eyewitness accounts, Robert McKinnon shows how the Jacobite cause slowly gathered strength, beginning with the campaign of "Bonnie Dundee" in 1689, and explains how the British Government's acts of cruelty, such as the Massacre of Glencoe, only strengthened the Highlanders' resolve to continue their struggle. He describes in detail the "Forty-Five" campaign of Bonnie Prince Charlie which ended in his defeat at Culloden and escape to France. It had cost the lives of thousands of brave clansmen and "redcoat" soldiers, but he himself died in his bed in 1788, exactly one hundred years after his grandfather had been deposed.

This new DOCUMENTARY HISTORY title is illustrated with fifty contemporary prints.

The Jacobite Rebellions

Robert McKinnon

WAYLAND PUBLISHERS · LONDON

G. P. PUTNAM'S SONS · NEW YORK

Frontispiece The Battle of Culloden, 16th April, 1746

SBN 85340 272 8
Copyright © 1973 by Wayland (Publishers) Ltd
101 Grays Inn Road, London WC1
Set in 'Monophoto' Times and printed offset litho in Great Britain by
Page Bros (Norwich) Ltd. Norwich

Contents

The Illustrations

1 The Seeds of Rebellion

FOR MOST PEOPLE, the Jacobite Rebellion begins and ends with the famous story of Bonnie Prince Charlie. Yet the first uprising took place more than thirty years before he was born, while the roots of the Rebellion go back a further forty years to the English Civil War (1642–49). From that struggle England emerged roughly divided between the Puritan revolutionaries who supported Oliver Cromwell, and the royalists who remained faithful to the Stuart monarchy and to the memory of Charles I whom Cromwell had beheaded in Whitehall in January, 1649.

The word "Jacobite" became familiar to the people of *James II* England about the year 1688. King James II of England, who was also James VII of Scotland, had succeeded his brother Charles II, the Merry Monarch, in 1685. But, unlike Charles, there was nothing merry about James. He took life extremely seriously, especially in matters of religion. He was a fervent Roman Catholic convert in a land where most people were by now firmly anti-Catholic. It was widely feared that James might try to re-establish the Catholic faith as the official religion.

"The King was totally blind to the dangerous precipice on which he stood," wrote Sir Walter Scott, the famous Scottish novelist. "He imagined that the murmurs of the people might be suppressed by the large standing army which he maintained (1)."

In fact the army itself was quite indifferent to matters of religion. But if anything, most of the soldiery was anti-Catholic. Scott goes on to point out: "Any prince less obstinate and bigoted than James might easily have seen that the army would not become his instrument in altering the laws and religion of

9

Opposite James II with his second wife, Mary of Modena, and their two children James, the Old Pretender, and Louisa Maria Theresa the country. But he proceeded to provoke a struggle, which it was plain must be maintained against the universal sentiments of his subjects. He had the folly not only to set up Catholic worship in his royal chapel, with the greatest pomp and publicity, but to send an ambassador, Lord Castlemaine, to the Pope to invite His Holiness to countenance his proceedings by sending him a nuncio [envoy] from the See of Rome. Such a communication was, by the law of England, an act of high treason, and excited the deepest resentment (2).''

A Catholic heir

In June, 1688, things came to a crisis when James's second wife, Mary of Modena, gave birth to a son. The boy would almost certainly be brought up a Catholic – a prospect that alarmed most English people. They feared that the infant James might one day strengthen the Catholic hold on the monarchy. They had hoped that Mary, James's half-sister, would succeed him. Mary herself was the wife of the cold and ambitious Dutch Prince William of Orange, whom the English Protestants had come to look upon as their champion.

Protestant suspicions

The Catholic section of the population was delighted at the news of the Royal birth; but the Protestants, said Scott, "were disposed to consider the alleged birth of the infant, which had happened so seasonably for the Catholics, as the result not of a miracle of the Popish saints but of a trick at Court. They affirmed that the child was not really the son of James and his wife but a supposititious infant, whom they were desirous to palm upon their subjects as the legal heir of the throne in order to defeat the claim of the Protestant successors. This assertion, though gravely swallowed by the people and widely spread amongst them, was totally without foundation (3)."

Prince William was ill pleased to hear the news, "seeing himself by the birth and rights of this infant excluded from the long-hoped-for succession to the crown of England (4)."

William of Orange

So the scene was set for a confrontation; and it was not long in coming. It began when some of the leading British Protestant politicians and merchants invited Prince William of Orange to come over from Holland to help them prevent James from setting up a permanent Catholic monarchy. William responded gladly and quickly. He put to sea with an army of 15,000 men and a fleet of some 50 ships. He landed at Torbay in Devonshire, on 5th November, 1688, but claimed his only purpose in coming was to secure life, liberty and property in Britain from the evil counsellors of the King.

From other evidence available it is clear that William of Orange had long coveted the English throne; his statement at Torbay was therefore untrue. Be that as it may, more and more influential people began to join his cause. The defection even spread to King James's army assembled at Salisbury to fight the invaders. Several officers of high rank publicly deserted the King, among them Lord Churchill, who was later given the title of Duke of Marlborough. This particular desertion hurt the King a great deal, for Churchill had always been a favourite of his. It was James who had given him his peerage and his high rank in the army. *Churchill defects*

"A still more striking defection," Scott wrote, "seems to have destroyed the remains of the unhappy monarch's resolution. His second daughter, the Princess Anne, who was married to a younger son of the King of Denmark, called Prince George, escaped by night from London under the protection of the Bishop of that city, who raised a body of horse for her safeguard and rode armed at their head. She fled to Nottingham, where she was received by the Earl of Dorset, and declared for a free Protestant Parliament. Her husband, and other persons of the first distinction, joined the Prince of Orange . . .

"At the tidings of his daughter's flight, James exclaimed in an agony of personal feeling, 'God help me, my own children desert me' (5)."

During all this disturbance, the King had sent the rest of his family to France for safety. His own plans were to stay on in London, but these quickly changed after he had received an ultimatum from his son-in-law, William, to leave his Palace. James yielded to William's demand and left for Rochester. There, he embarked on a frigate bound for France and landed at Ambleteuse on 23rd December, 1688. He was received with the utmost hospitality by Louis XIV, the King of France, and lived under Louis's protection until his death in 1701. Throughout that time, James was to leave France only once, for a brief *Flight to France*

Overleaf William of Orange landing at Torbay on 5th November, 1688

After William landed, James II fled with his family to France

campaign against William of Orange in Ireland (1690).

Early in 1689 a Parliamentary Convention was called at Westminster. After much argument, it was declared that King James II had abdicated and that the throne was vacant.

The succession settlement Because William held so much power and influence, "The Convention were obliged to regulate the succession to the throne upon the terms agreeable to the Prince of Orange. The Princess and he were called to the throne jointly, under the title of King William and Queen Mary, the survivor succeeding the party who should first die. The Princess Anne of Denmark was named to succeed after the death of her sister and brother-in-law, and the claims of James's infant son were entirely passed over (6)."

14

Opposite Louis XIV welcomes James II to the French court

La Reine d'Angleterre attendant le Roy son Espoux

William and Mary receiving the Crown of England

At the same time as the Crown was given to William and Mary, the Convention also took the opportunity of issuing a special Declaration of Rights defining the future limits of royal authority. It insisted that from now on the monarchy must yield to Parliament in all matters affecting the life and liberties of the English people.

Such, then, were the main events of what became known as the "Glorious Revolution" of 1688–89. Certainly it was a great landmark in the rise of Parliamentary power. But those who

believed that a major victory had been won without bloodshed were to be proved totally wrong. Many people in Britain, by no means all of them Catholic, still looked on James as the rightful monarch; William was the "Dutch usurper." They became known as "Jacobites" – that is, supporters of the exiled King James. The term comes from *Jacobus,* the Latin form of James. They were to go on fighting for the Stuart cause long after the death of James himself.

John Graham of Claverhouse, popularly known as "Bonnie Dundee,"
led a rising in support of James II in 1689

2 *The First Uprising*

The Jacobite Rebellions

IN ALL, there were five Jacobite uprisings in Britain over the fifty-seven years that followed the "Glorious Revolution." Two of them – those of 1708 and 1719 – were abortive, and in the end gave the Whig Government in London little or no trouble. Any of the other three, however, had they not been dogged by sheer bad luck or by plain bad judgement, might have restored the Stuart king to the British throne.

"Bonnie Dundee"

The first of the uprisings erupted in Scotland a few months after William and Mary were made King and Queen. Its central character was a gay and dashing Scottish noble, John Graham of Claverhouse, Viscount Dundee, whose dark good looks earned him the name of "Bonnie Dundee." Dundee had been a devoted friend and supporter of King James as well as one of his ablest followers. And it is said that, upon hearing of the King's flight to France, he "with the Lords Linlithgow and Dunmore shed tears of grief and mortification (7)."

At this time Scotland was an independent country with its own Parliament (or Convention) and tied to England only through the Union of the Crowns when James VI of Scotland came to the English throne in 1603. Soon after James II's flight to the court of Louis XIV, the Scottish Parliament held a meeting in Edinburgh. Dundee urged the members to fight for James. The same plea was celebrated in Sir Walter Scott's famous song, *Bonnie Dundee* (8):

> *To the Lords of Convention 'twas Claverhouse spoke,*
> *Ere the King's crown go down there are crowns to be broke,*

19

So each Cavalier who loves honour and me
Let him follow the bonnets of Bonnie Dundee

Then awa' to the hills, to the lea, to the rocks,
Ere I own a usurper I'll crouch wi' the fox,
And tremble false Whigs in the midst of your glee
You've no seen the last of my bonnets and me

The Scottish Parliament, however, could not make up its mind whether to support James or William, but finally it came down timorously on the side of William. Meanwhile, a letter had been intercepted showing the extent of Dundee's loyalty and support for James, and he was summoned from his country home near the port of Dundee to answer for his opinions before the Scottish authorities in Edinburgh.

Highland chieftains   P. Hume-Brown, a Scottish historian, tells what happened: "Dundee refused to obey the summons. And, on an attempt being made to capture him by surprise, he took refuge in the depths of the Highlands. Fortune now brought him precisely the occasion he could have wished for the display of his special gifts of mind and character. To the cause of James he was bound alike by instinct and interest, and for various reasons a numerous group of Highland chiefs were now as eager to draw the sword for James as they had been for his father, Charles I, during the Civil War . . . Among those who joined him when he presented himself as the Lieutenant-General of King James were the Captain of Clanranald, MacDonald of Sleat, Maclean of Dowart, Stewart of Appin, Cameron of Lochiel, Glengarry, MacDonald of Keppoch, MacNeil of Barra and MacDonald of Glencoe (9)."

The Highland chieftains did not rally to the Jacobite cause purely out of a sense of loyalty and affection for the exiled monarch. One of their reasons was fear of losing land given to them when James was Commissioner for Scotland during the reign of Charles II (1660–85). In particular, much of this land had once been part of the estates of the Duke of Argyll, the powerful chief of the Clan Campbell.

The Campbells   The Clan Campbell had been a kind of "back sheep" in the whole clan system almost since time immemorial. But it was very strong and influential. It had supported Oliver Cromwell during the Civil War; the Campbells were Presbyterian, and enjoyed the support of the Whig Government in London. To the Jacobites, the name of Campbell was a curse, especially to neighbouring clans such as the Camerons, MacDonalds, MacPhersons, Robertsons and Stewarts.

The task of suppressing Dundee's uprising had been given to one of William's best and most resolute officers, Major-General Hugh MacKay. The two armies met on 27th July, 1689, at the Pass of Killiecrankie – a wild but beautiful part of Atholl in north-west Perthshire. According to Hume-Brown: *Battle of Killiecrankie*

"For strategy there was little hope on either side, but from the nature of Dundee's troops the advantage of the ground was all in his favour. MacKay had at his disposal some 3,000 foot [soldiers] and four troops of horse – the latter of little avail against such an enemy on a rough and steep mountainside. Dundee had between 2,000 and 3,000 foot [soldiers], including about 300 men from Ireland, which was largely Jacobite, and one troop of cavalry. About half an hour from sunset the Highlanders rapidly descended the hill. Against their headlong onset the troops of MacKay were at a hopeless disadvantage. Many of them were untrained levies, and their weapons had never been proved against such agile foes. Before they could fix their bayonets after discharging their fire, their line was broken and three-fourths of their ranks were in hopeless confusion (10)."

Fortunately for the Government, luck was with MacKay's men in their struggle with the Jacobites. As Hume-Brown explains: "Two circumstances saved MacKay from utter ruin. True to their inveterate habit, the Highlanders no sooner saw themselves masters of the field than they fell upon the spoils; and under cover of night MacKay was able to cross the Garry with the feeble remnant of his host. Still more fortunately for the defeated commander, his victorious antagonist fell in the first onset of the battle, and his death turned a brilliant advantage into a fatal disaster (11)."

The manner in which Dundee died stirred many a Jacobite *Death of a hero*

21

A contemporary print showing William III's victory over the forces of
James Stuart at the Battle of the Boyne, 1690

breast. One of the most famous poets of the day, John Dryden, wrote this in his honour (12):

> O last and best of Scots! who didst maintain
> Thy country's freedom from a foreign race;
> New people fill the land, now they are gone;
> New Gods the temples and new Kings the throne;
> Scotland and thou did in each other live,
> Thou couldst not her nor could she thee survive;
> Farewell, that living didst support the state,
> And couldst not fall but by thy country's fate.

It may be thought that the forces of William of Orange were extraordinarily lucky in that one of their bullets should have struck Dundee in his hour of triumph. The following explanation of his death, from James Hogg's *The Jacobite Relics of Scotland*, is therefore of much interest. One thing to remember is that during the reign of Charles II, Graham of Claverhouse had been the bitter foe of the Scottish Covenanters (the devout Presbyterians who had long opposed the House of Stuart). "From my youth," wrote Hogg, "I have heard a tradition that Dundee fell by the hand of his own servant; and I have heard it so often, and with so many attendant circumstances, that I believe it.

Clavers's revenge   "This servant is said to have been a Covenanter of Lanarkshire, whose whole kin Clavers had murdered on account of their tenets. And this remaining stem had taken an oath to his God to be revenged by shedding the blood of that detested persecutor, or to perish in the attempt. For that purpose he followed him, first as a volunteer and afterwards was employed about him as a groom. In these capacities he had watched his opportunities for three years and a half. But he could never find a chance of executing his purpose with any prospect of safety for himself, until the hottest of the battle of Killiecrankie, when he shot him below the arm with a horse pistol charged with a silver button instead of a bullet, as he believed in the popular superstition that Clavers was proof against lead.

"This feat, it is said, the incendiary used to boast of as long as he lived. It has likewise been said that Clavers was shot by a gentleman who was in love with his lady, and to whom she was

24

James II fleeing to France after the defeat at the Battle of the Boyne

very shortly married. Both may be alike untrue (13)."

With Dundee dead, the Highlanders did not pose much of a threat to the Government in London – formidable though they were in battle. During the winter of 1689–90, the exiled King James tried once more to rally the clansmen to his side. Some clans did respond, but on 1st May, 1690, they were literally caught napping by a detachment of William's army at Cromdale on the banks of the River Spey. The surprised Highlanders fought gallantly, but were put to flight.

Weeks later, in Ireland, King William's army smashed the army of James Stuart at the now famous Battle of the Boyne. This marked the end of the first Jacobite attempt to restore the Stuarts. But though campaigns had been lost, the cause continued to flourish.

Battle of the Boyne

Indeed, it was soon helped by a crime committed in the name of William of Orange which, for sheer cruelty, has rarely been matched in these islands.

3 The Jacobite Cause Gains Strength

THE DEED was the infamous Massacre of Glencoe. It took place in the early hours of the morning of 13th February, 1692. The events leading up to it were as follows.

After the battle at Cromdale actual warfare in the Highlands came to an end, but it was an uneasy peace. Many chieftains still felt strongly for King James, and were persuaded that a French force might land at almost any time on the west coast of Scotland. Evidently the Government in London was also ready to believe this, for it set aside the sum of £12,000 to buy a promise from the same chieftains to remain at peace with King William. The Earl of Breadalbane, head of one of the many Campbell clans, and said to be a man as "cunning as a fox, wise as a serpent and slippery as an eel," was chosen to supervise this particular piece of bribery. *An uneasy peace*

There is no doubt that Breadalbane kept much of the £12,000 for himself and his friends. Also, some of the chiefs refused to swear an oath to keep the peace. Some of them felt the price was too low, and others – men of honour – stayed loyal to King James. So to back up the bribe, a proclamation was issued by the Privy Council. It required the chiefs to sign an oath of allegiance to King William by 1st January, 1692, and the "utmost extremity of the law" would be used against any chieftain who did not sign. *Oath of allegiance*

The man behind this plan was Sir John Dalrymple, Master of Stair and a member of the Scottish Privy Council. Dalrymple came to be loathed and feared throughout the length and breadth of Scotland. To this day, the playing card, the Nine of Diamonds, *"The Curse of Scotland"*

The Massacre of Glencoe, 1692, was one of the most brutal episodes in English military history is sometimes called "The Curse of Scotland" because of its resemblance to the Dalrymple coat of arms. In any case, Dalrymple was both a trusted servant of William and a trusted friend of Breadalbane.

Hume-Brown claims: "It was with a sense of disappointment that Dalrymple learned that all the chieftains with the exception of MacIan [chief of the Clan MacDonald of Glencoe] had taken the oath by the appointed day. In the case of most of them he was convinced that the oath was an idle form, and that the only security against their future rebellion was to cow them by a few terrible examples."

The "damnable" MacDonalds

It was with undisguised rejoicing, therefore, that he heard of MacDonald's failure to give the necessary satisfaction. If only one chief was to be taught a lesson, MacIan was the victim he would have desired most. The clan was a "thieving tribe, a damnable sept, the worst in all the Highlands; its chief had fought under Dundee at Killiecrankie and was deep in every Highland plot against the Government (14)."

Like most of the Highland clans, the MacDonalds of Glencoe were no angels. They had committed their full share of cattle stealing and blood spilling, but in their dealings with others they did at least observe a rough code of honour. This apart, MacIan did not refuse to sign the oath of allegiance, but merely left the signing to the eleventh hour.

Shortly before the 1st January, the old chief rode with his principal followers to Fort William to take the oath of allegiance. Here "he was much alarmed to find that Colonel Hill, the governor of Fort William, had no power to receive it, being a military and not a civil officer (15)." Colonel Hill, however, sympathized with the old chieftain and gave him a letter to take to Sir Colin Campbell, Sheriff of Argyllshire, at Inveraray:

"MacIan hastened from Fort William to Inveraray without even turning aside to his own house, though he passed within a mile of it. But the roads, always very bad, were now rendered almost impassable by a storm of snow. So that, with all the speed the unfortunate chieftain could exert, the fatal 1st of January was past before he reached Inveraray.

MacIan takes the oath

"The Sheriff, however, seeing that MacIan had complied with

the spirit of the statute . . . did not hesitate to administer the oath of allegiance, and sent off an express [message] to the Privy Council containing an attestation of MacIan's having taken the oath, and a full explanation of the circumstances which had delayed his doing so until the lapse of the appointed period. The Sherriff also wrote to Colonel Hill and requested that Glencoe should not be annoyed by any military parties until the pleasure of the Council should be known, which he could not doubt would be favourable (16)."

Mysteriously, the letter from the Sheriff to the Privy Council never arrived. Or was it a mystery? Where a man like Dalrymple was concerned a great deal could be concluded. Especially when he wrote in a royal warrant drafted on 16th January, 1692, "As for MacIan of Glencoe and that tribe, if they can be well distinguished from the rest of the Highlanders, it will be proper for the vindication of public justice to extirpate that set of thieves (17)."

Certainly, Dalrymple's letters to his military officers leave no doubt as to the kind of man he was. "The winter," he wrote to one of them, "is the only season in which the Highlanders cannot elude us, or carry their wives, children and cattle to the mountains. They cannot escape you. For what human constitution can then endure to be long out of house? This is the proper season to maul them, in the long dark nights . . . To plunder their lands or drive off their cattle would be only to render them desperate. They must all be slaughtered, and the manner of execution must be sure, secret and effectual (18)."

Dalrymple's ruthlessness

Imagine, then, Dalrymple's barely concealed delight at the "news" of MacIan MacDonald breaking the time limit for taking the oath of allegiance to King William. Moreover, he had no difficulty in finding people willing to organize the butchering of civilians. Those in charge of the "operation" were Major Robert Duncanson and his subordinate, Captain Robert Campbell of Glenlyon.

And so, towards the end of January, 1692, Glenlyon arrived at Glencoe with a troop of 120 men, among them many Campbells. Most of his troops were in fact Highlanders, and they lived "familiarly with MacIan and his people" – in other words, enjoyed their hospitality – until 13th February.

On the 12th, Glenlyon had received the orders from Duncanson: "You are hereby ordered to fall upon the rebels and put all to the sword under seventy. You are to have especial care that the old fox and his cubs do on no account escape your hands. You are to secure all the avenues, that no man escape. This you are to put in execution at four in the morning precisely . . . By that time, or very shortly after, I will strive to be at you with a stronger party. But if I do not come to you at four, you are not to tarry for me, but fall on (19)."

Massacre of Glencoe

Glenlyon carried out his orders to the letter, good soldier that he was! At four o'clock in the morning, he and his men rushed upon their sleeping hosts, butchering in all thirty-eight of the MacDonalds of Glencoe, including two children, two women and one old man of eighty.

This is an account of the atrocity: "The work of death proceeded with as little remorse as Stair himself could have desired. Even the slight mitigation of their orders regarding those above seventy years of age was disregarded by the soldiery in their indiscriminate thirst for blood . . . Several very aged and bedridden persons were slain amongst others. At the hamlet where Glenlyon had his own quarters, nine men, including his landlord, were bound and shot like felons . . .

"A fine lad of twenty, by some glimpse of compassion on the part of the soldiers, had been spared, when one Captain Drummond came up and, demanding why his orders were transgressed in that particular, caused him instantly to be put to death. A boy of five or six years old clung to Glenlyon's knees, entreating for mercy and offering to become his servant for life, if he would spare him. Glenlyon was moved; but the same Drummond stabbed the child with his dirk while he was in this agony of supplication (20)."

A whitewashing commission

Not until 1695 was a formal Commission of Enquiry set up to look into the Massacre, and find out who was to blame. Needless to say, it was a whitewashing body, which slurred over King William's part in it by saying that the Master of Stair's instructions went far beyond the terms of the warrant which the monarch had signed. Stair himself was sacked from his office of Secretary of State for Scottish Affairs, while Breadalbane was charged with high treason and imprisoned in Edinburgh Castle. But he was never brought to trial. As for Duncanson and Glenlyon, by the time the Commission was set up, they were on military service in Europe and as such regarded as beyond the reach of the law.

Escape for some

The only redeeming feature of this appalling massacre was the escape of about 150 of the MacDonalds into the recesses of their mountains in the winter darkness. And for those who supported the Jacobite cause, the Massacre of Glencoe did at least attract a great deal of sympathy. It may seem callous to talk about the propaganda value of an episode such as this, but it serves no purpose to blink at the cold facts.

The Darien Scheme

Further fuel for the Jacobite cause came three years after Glencoe in 1695 with the launching of a project known as the Darien Scheme. This was an attempt to set up a Scottish trading colony at Darien, the isthmus of land separating the continent of South America from that of North America. In those days, of course, there was no Panama Canal.

English fears

The Scheme was launched in July, 1695, with the setting up in Edinburgh of "The Company of Scotland Trading to Africa and the Indies." It had a capital of £600,000 – half of it coming from Scottish and half from English investors. Gradually, however, the English Parliament and merchants came to fear that the Company would capture most of their trade with India and the East. Parliament sent an address to King William voicing this very complaint. Back came a royal answer agreeing that "the King had been ill served in Scotland, but hoped some remedies might still be found to prevent the evils apprehended." William was even angrier at the thought that a Scottish colony in Darien would threaten the trade of his beloved Holland with the East Indies.

The expedition under way

Despite William's hostility, the Darien expedition left the harbour of Leith (Edinburgh's port) on the 17th July, 1698. It sailed "amidst the tears and prayers and praises of the whole city of Edinburgh." Three armed vessels sailed, *Caledonia*, *Unicorn* and *St. Andrew*, together with two supply ships. In addition to a cargo including periwigs and Bibles, there were: "Twelve hundred men, three hundred of whom were youths of the best Scottish families. They embarked on board of five frigates, purchased at Hamburg for the service of the expedition; for the King refused the Company even the trifling accommodation of a ship of war, which lay idle at Burntisland . . .

Caledonia

"They reached their destination in safety, and disembarked at a place called Acta, where, by cutting through a peninsula, they obtained a safe and insulated situation for a town, called New Edinburgh, and a fort named Saint Andrew. With the same fond remembrance of their native land, the colony itself was called Caledonia. They were favourably received by the native princes, from whom they purchased the land they required. The harbour, which was excellent, was proclaimed a free port and in the outset the happiest results were expected from the settlement (21)."

Disease and hostility

Apart from King William's hostility, there was also the problem that the Isthmus of Darien was rife with tropical diseases; in particular, the drinking water was badly infected. Also, the local Spanish settlers claimed that Darien belonged to them, and began to harass the Scots on land and sea, actively encouraged by the English court and Parliament. Thirdly, the governors of the English colonies in the West Indies were told by Whitehall to refuse all help to the Scots, and especially not to provide them with the much-needed supplies.

As one Scottish writer of the time said: "The more generous savages, by hunting and fishing for the Scots colonists, gave them that relief which fellow Britons refused (22)."

Failure of Darien

But the situation was hopeless. In June, 1699 – less than a year after it had left with such high hopes from Leith – the first Darien expedition sailed for home. The graves of three hundred men who had sailed with the expedition from Scotland were left behind as a tragic monument.

Two more Darien expeditions were planned for the years that followed. But these, too, were defeated by a combination of disasters, either at sea, or through Spanish attacks and English indifference, or simply from tropical diseases. The only bright interlude in an otherwise dark story took place in February, 1700, when two hundred Scots soldiers, with the aid of some local Indians, routed a Spanish force many times their number

An early map of the Isthmus of Darien, where Scottish merchants
hoped to set up a trading colony

who were closing in on the settlement.

A disastrous enterprise A few weeks later, Spanish pressure on the colony became much stronger, and the Scots were offered the kind of bargain that they could honourably accept. They would be allowed to leave Darien in their own ships "with colours flying and drums beating, together with their arms and ammunition and with all their goods." So on 11th April, 1700, the Scots left Darien for good. The enterprise had cost the mother country nearly 2,000 of her finest men and more than £200,000 in money. This sum may not sound much today, but it was money Scotland could ill afford at the time.

On 6th September, 1701, at St. Germain in France, the exiled King James II died at the age of sixty-seven. William, his son-in-law, followed him to the grave six months later, dying of pneumonia on 8th March, 1702, aged fifty-one. Queen Mary had died seven years before.

Queen Anne King William was succeeded by Anne, Mary's younger sister. Queen Anne was the daughter of James II by his first wife, Anne Hyde. Strictly on the principle of male succession, Anne's half-brother James – the son of James II by his second wife Mary of Modena – had a prior claim to the British crown.

"The Old Pretender" The young James was only thirteen when Anne came to the throne. In time he became known as "The Old Pretender" to distinguish him from his son, Prince Charles, who acquired such a romantic reputation as "The Young Pretender." In his day the Old Pretender was regarded by many people in Britain as the rightful monarch and was known by them as "James III of England and VIII of Scotland." Here, he will be referred to from time to time as "The Old Pretender" and sometimes as "James."

The word "pretender" does not mean that the person is a confidence trickster. Rather, it derives from the French word *prétendant*, meaning claimant. Indeed, nobody has ever had a better claim to the British throne than James III, and still been denied it.

The Act of Union So much, then, for the dynastic background. A new event now put the cat among the pigeons for Anglo-Scottish relations. This was the Act of Union (1707). The law was carried through

34

An engraving of the Old Pretender (*top*) and some of his principal followers

the Scottish Parliament against bitter opposition, both inside Parliament and among ordinary Scottish people. The Act effectively joined Scotland and England by merging its Parliament with the one at Westminster. Even today it is still a topic of resentment and protest among Scottish Nationalists.

The Union was not achieved without protest. The final session of the last Scottish Parliament began on 3rd October, 1706, and a month later the proposed Treaty of Union was still being angrily debated.

"Shall we in half an hour yield what our forefathers maintained with their lives and fortunes for many ages?" asked the Duke of Hamilton. "Are none of the descendants here of those worthy patriots who defended the liberty of their country against all invaders, who assisted the great King Robert Bruce to restore the constitution and avenge the falsehood of England? Where are the Douglases and the Campbells? Where are the peers, where are the barons – once the bulwark of the nation – when we are commanded by those we represent to preserve the name of Scotland? (23)" Hamilton's speech even brought tears to the eyes of Members of Parliament who supported the idea of union.

Meanwhile, the people of the country had shown where their feelings lay: "The unpopularity of the proposed measure throughout Scotland in general," wrote Sir Walter Scott, "was soon made evident by the temper of the people of Edinburgh . . . On the 23rd of October the popular fury was at its height. The people crowded together in the High Street and Parliament Square, and greeted their representatives as friends or enemies to their country, according as they opposed or favoured the Union. The Commissioner was bitterly reviled . . .

"At the evening of the day, several hundred persons escorted the Duke of Hamilton to his lodgings, encouraging him by loud huzzas to stand by the cause of national independence. The rabble next assailed the house of the Lord Provost, destroyed the windows and broke open the doors, and threatened him with instant death as a favourer of the obnoxious treaty (24)."

The story is now taken up by George Lockhart of Carnwath, a Scottish writer of the time. Lockhart supported the Jacobite cause, but he was a truthful and fair-minded reporter of the facts: "About three hundred or four hundred of the mob, as soon as they left His Grace of Hamilton, did hasten in a body to the house of Sir Patrick Johnstone, their late darling Provost, who sat as one of the representatives of Edinburgh in Parliament. They searched his house for him. But he, having narrowly made his escape, prevented his being torn into a thousand pieces. From thence the mob, which was increased to a great number, went through the streets threatening destruction to all the promoters of the Union, and continued for four or five hours in this temper . . . (25)"

English bribes

Lockhart added that these riots, as well as other evidence, made it clear that "the Union was crammed down Scotland's throat." There is ample evidence to confirm the Jacobite's charge that English gold was used as a sweetener to get the Act "down Scotland's throat" and it was no malicious rumour. Bribery was used in the right quarters, though the extent was probably much exaggerated.

Here is a Jacobite song which was written to lament the passing of the Act of Union:

Fareweel to a' our Scottish fame.
Fareweel our ancient glory.
Fareweel even to the Scottish name.
Sae famed in martial story.
Now Sark rins o'er the Solway strand
And Tweed rins to the ocean
To mark where England's province stands –
Such a parcel of rogues in a nation.

What force or guile could not subdue
Through many warlike ages,
Is wrought now by a coward few
For hireling traitors' wages
The English steel we could disdain
Secure in valour's station,
But English gold has been our bane –
Such a parcel of rogues in a nation.

37

Overleaf Queen Anne is presented with the Articles of Union, which joined England and Scotland, in 1707

No matter how the votes were obtained, Queen Anne gave the royal assent to the Treaty of Union on 6th March, 1707. As Hume-Brown explains, on the 19th of that month "amid a salvo of guns from the [Edinburgh] Castle the Act was read to the Scottish Parliament and ordered to be recorded. As the Chancellor Seafield handed the Act, with his signature affixed, to the Clerk of the House, he is said to have exclaimed, 'Now, there's ane end of ane auld song'."

It may have been the end of an old song, but its tune was to have one or two strident echoes before it died away for all time.

The Union provided the fuel. The spark lay in the traditional friendship between Scotland and France. The two countries had held an "auld alliance" since the fourteenth century when thousands of Scots went to Europe as mercenaries in the Hundred Years' War. This alliance was cemented by a formal treaty in 1548 when a French force relieved a number of Scottish strongholds under siege by the English. "France and Scotland are now one country," exclaimed Henry II of France when the treaty was signed.

In fact, the old alliance between Scotland and France was based more on a common fear and dislike of England than on mutual affection. Contact between the two peoples was not always friendly. One case in point was the street fighting in Edinburgh between the French and the townspeople when the treaty was announced in 1548. On the other hand, Louis XIV of France, as we shall see, seems to have been a very good friend of the Stuarts.

4 The Fight for the Old Pretender

THE YEAR 1708 gave the Jacobites their best chance of putting a Stuart back on the throne. But through timidity and sheer bad luck, they bungled it hopelessly. This is how it happened.

After the Union of 1707, Scotland was not a happy country. *Scottish* *grievances* It seemed as if every section of society north of the border had some real grievance against the Treaty. The relationship between the two countries was not helped by Harley, the English Secretary of State, who had done much to get the Treaty signed. For Harley asked in Parliament: "Have we not bought the Scots, and did we not acquire the right to tax them?"

Sir Walter Scott explains how the Scots felt at the time: *A coalition* "The detestation of the Treaty being for the present the ruling passion of the times," he wrote, "all other distinctions of party, and even of religious opinion in Scotland, were laid aside . . . A singular coalition took place, in which Episcopalians, Presbyterians, Cavaliers and many friends of the Revolution drowned all former hostility. Even the Cameronians, who now formed a powerful body in the state, retained the same zeal against the Union when established, which had induced them to rise in arms in support of it while it was in progress (26)."

Lockhart in his *Papers* tells how only a Scottish king could *A Scottish* *king?* restore the Scots their rights: "People of all ranks and persuasions were more and more chagrined and displeased, so that nothing but the restoration of the royal family – and that by means of Scotsmen – could restore to them their rights. So that there was now scarce one in a thousand who did not declare for the King [the nineteen-year-old James III and VIII].

Louis XIV holds a reception at St. Germain

Nay, the Presbyterians and Cameronians were willing to pass over the objection of his being Papist. 'For,' said they, 'God may convert him, or he may have Protestant children, but the Union can never be made good' (27)."

Reports of this kind soon reached the ears of Louis XIV of France who at the time was fighting England on the Continent in the War of the Spanish Succession. John Churchill, Duke of Marlborough, was costing England a great deal in terms of blood and treasure. On the other hand, he was gaining major victories against the French. What could suit Louis better than an uprising in Scotland?

Louis XIV's *spy*

As a first step, Louis sent a special agent to spy out the land and gauge the strength of feeling in Scotland for the Jacobite cause. The agent was Lieutenant-Colonel Hooke, an Englishman of good family who had been a devoted follower of James II. Finally, after much delay, Louis decided to send the young

James to Scotland with an invasion fleet and 5,000 men to help him win back the British throne.

Admiral Forbin was placed in charge of the French invasion force, though he was by no means keen on the plan nor confident of its outcome. He is reported to have said to the French War Minister, "You have 5,000 troops to throw away on a desperate expedition. Give me command of them. I will embark them in shallops and light vessels, and I will surprise Amsterdam and, by destroying the commerce of the Dutch capital, take away all means and desire on the part of the United Provinces to continue the war. But this venture is sheer folly." The Minister, however, quickly reminded Forbin that he "was called upon to execute the King's commands, not to discuss them." *A French invasion fleet*

By all accounts Forbin exaggerated the dangers that confronted him. Most of the English army was fighting the French in Flanders, and had at home only 5,000 raw recruits. The Scottish defences were in an even worse state as there were less than 2,000 Government troops in the whole of the country.

Early in March, 1708, a French invasion force began to assemble at Dunkirk under the command of Admiral Forbin, with the Comte de Gasse in charge of the land forces. They were joined by the Chevalier de St. George (the French title for the young James) who immediately contracted measles and delayed the date of sailing for several days.

Scott describes the scene: "Twelve battalions were embarked on board of eight ships of the line and twenty-four frigates, besides transports and shallops for disembarkation. The King of France displayed his magnificence by supplying the Chevalier de St. George with a royal wardrobe, services of gold and silver plate, rich liveries for his attendants, splendid uniforms for his guards and all external appurtenances [trappings] befitting the rank of a sovereign prince (28)."

The expedition sailed from Dunkirk on 17th March, but they were held up for a further two days by an unfavourable wind. At length, however, they reached the Firth of Forth on the east coast of Scotland and dropped anchor off Crail, a little fishing village on the Fife coast. *The expedition sets sail*

Admiral Forbin wrote of the voyage: James "arrived at

Dunkirk, but fell ill of measles and was for two days in a fever. The delay which his illness caused allowed the enemy time to reconnoitre our position. Thirty-eight English men-of-war anchored off Gravelines, two leagues from Dunkirk. Later, the wind becoming favourable, we set sail, and on the third day were off the coast of Scotland in sight of land. But our pilots had made an error of six leagues in their bearings [which would explain their anchoring off Crail] so we altered course and, the wind and tide becoming contrary, anchored at nightfall at the mouth of the Edinburgh River [the Firth of Forth].

"In vain we made signals, lit fires and fired our cannon. Nobody appeared. At daybreak we discovered the English fleet had anchored at four leagues' distance from us, and the sight of them caused me considerable uneasiness. We were shut in a sort of bay, with a cape to be doubled before we could gain the open sea (29)."

James demanded that he and his attendants be put ashore at Wemyss Castle on the Fife Coast, the seat of the Earl of Wemyss whose family had long backed the Stuart cause. But Admiral Forbin replied: "Sire, by the orders of my royal master, I am directed to take the same precautions for the safety of your august person as for His Majesty's own. This must be my chief care. You are at present in safety, and I will never consent to your being exposed in a ruinous chateau in an open country, where a few hours might put you in the hands of your enemies. I am entrusted with your person and am answerable for your safety with my head. I beseech you, therefore, to repose your confidence in me entirely and to listen to no one else (30)."

James sails away

Whether James was worried about Admiral Forbin's head, or swayed by the wisdom of his plea, we do not know. In any event he sailed away from the coast of Scotland when a little daring and imagination might have won him the throne of Great Britain and Ireland.

Initially at least, very little defence could have been mustered against James. The Earl of Leven, commander of the Scottish forces, could raise only two or three regiments, and when writing to the Secretary of State for Scotland he said that the Jacobites in Edinburgh were "in such numbers and show themselves so elated that I dare scarce look them in the face as I walk the streets (31)."

Testimony to this is borne out by a report from a Jacobite supporter on how Edinburgh received the news of James's sudden arrival and even more abrupt departure: "Never was seen so universal a joy as that which was seen in everybody's countenance. The loyal subjects thronged together, and those of the Government durst not appear in public. They had no confidence in the regular troops, knowing that the best part, both of the officers and the soldiers, were well-affected to the King. Besides, there was neither powder nor ammunition in the Castle of Edinburgh, nor in that of Stirling; and they knew that all the gentry would revolt from the Government the moment the King landed . . . But no sooner was it known by the gazettes that the King was returned to Dunkirk, than the consternation was so great that everybody appeared distracted (32)."

Edinburgh's joy

Perhaps it was due to the combination of bad weather and James's hesitancy, or of Forbin's concern for James's neck, that Queen Anne remained Queen of Scotland. But whatever the reason, the Scots' first attempt to put James on the throne had failed.

Queen Anne died on 1st August, 1714. Her death occurred before she could appoint Lord Bolingbroke Prime Minister and Lord Treasurer, as had been her intention. A few days before her death, however, the Whig Ministers in Parliament, who claimed they were acting in Anne's name, conferred the post on the Duke of Somerset, and obtained her agreement while she was too weak and tired to resist.

The Uprising of 1715

The Whigs lost no time in assembling Parliament. They quickly proclaimed as sovereign a German princeling, George, Elector of Hanover, and sent to Germany for him to come and occupy the throne without delay. George's claim as the "rightful sovereign" rested on the fact that he was the grandson of Elizabeth, daughter of James I of England and VI of Scotland. Elizabeth married the Elector of Palatine (Palatine was a German principality) and their daughter Sophia married the Elector of Hanover. George himself was fifty-four when he

George I

The reception of George I at St. James's Palace, September, 1714

received the message from the Whigs. He landed at Greenwich to take up the throne on 17th September, 1714.

The new sovereign was unable to speak English, and had very little tact, or understanding of how things were done in Britain. He became more of a Whig leader than a monarch to all his people.

George's tastes were those of a European peasant. Legend has it that he was working in his vegetable garden when told that he was to be the new King of Great Britain. The Jacobites noted the event in a satirical song (33):

> *Wha the deil hae we gotten for a king*
> *But a wee, wee German lairdie;*
> *And when we gade to bring him hame,*
> *He was delving in his kail-yardie.*
> *Sleughing kail and laying leeks*
> *Without the hose and but the breeks*
> *And up his begger duds he cleeks,*
> *The wee, wee German lairdie . . .*

The song goes on to deplore many things about the "wee German lairdie," but particularly the new language at the Court (34):

> *Auld Scotland, thou'rt o'er cauld a hole*
> *For nursing siccan vermin,*
> *But the very dogs o' England's court*
> *They bark and howl in German.*

Although George received a full official welcome, including fireworks, illuminations, and the ringing of bells and gun salutes, these "demonstrations of extraordinary joy" concealed the fact that the whole nation was in a state of seething unrest. The Whigs well knew that sympathy for James was widespread and in many cases went very deep. So, before George had set foot in England, they offered a £100,000 reward for James's capture.

The unrest was greatest of all in the Highlands where, during most of 1714, the clans had been indulging in all kinds of gestures. "In July 1715," wrote Hume-Brown, "the state of things in both countries became so menacing that on the 20th of that month the King formally announced to the House of Commons that the country was in danger and that preparations were necessary to avert it. There was an enthusiastic response on the part both of Lords and Commons; the Habeas Corpus Act and the Scottish Act corresponding to it were suspended, and the offer of £100,000 for the person of the Pretender was renewed. Against invasion the fleet and army were put on a war footing. Twenty-one regiments were raised, and the train-bands [local militia] ordered to be ready for emergencies (35)."

At this point an unsavoury but remarkable character enters the story. John, Earl of Mar was his name, a Scottish nobleman of the time known to everyone as "Bobbing John" because of his habit of changing sides. It is hard to sum up his career in a few words, but Hume-Brown tells us: "He had been a Privy Councillor under King William; he had been an ardent adherent of Queensberry in the reign of Anne, had deserted him and re-joined him. He was one of the principal agents in effecting the Union, but had soon changed his mind and professed to regret his action. He had been in communication with the Pretender for four years before the death of Anne, yet none was more enthusiastic in the expression of his loyalty at the accession of the Hanoverian King (36)." *"Bobbing John"*

On 2nd August, Mar left Gravesend for Scotland in a coal boat, having been snubbed by "the wee German lairdie" at a *levée* – morning audience – the day before. He landed in Fife and went at once to his own estates in Braemar to start gathering the clans in support of James. The meeting took place under the pretext of a grand hunting party on 26th August. Many great Scottish nobles arrived, and those unable to come sent repre-sentatives. The gathering is celebrated in another Jacobite song (37): *Meeting of the clans*

> *The Standard on the braes of Mar,*
> *Is up and streaming rarely,*
> *The gathering pipe on Lochnagar,*
> *Is sounding loud and clearly.*
> *The Hieland men frae hill and glen,*
> *Wi' belted plaids and glittering blades,*
> *Wi' bonnets blue and hearts sae true*

Seeds of rebellion

The clans agreed to go into battle for the Old Pretender as soon as the time was ripe. In the meantime, they continued to plan for the capture of Edinburgh Castle. The plan failed, but had it succeeded, James might have gained Scotland without a major battle as nearly all the country's ammunition was stored in the Castle. Fifty specially picked men had been chosen for the raid and one or two guards inside the Castle bribed to help them enter. However, the plan was betrayed by the sister-in-law of one of the conspirators and the guards paid the penalty with their lives.

James Rae, a soldier in the Government army, wrote afterwards that the main traitor was "William Ainslie, a sergeant, who hath since been hanged for his villainy. [He] had the promise of a lieutenant's place; and James Thomson and John Holland, two single sentinels, had received, the one eight guineas, and the other, four, with the promise of a better reward if the design should succeed. And it hath since appeared by their own confession that the numbers engaged in this attempt were about eighty, besides officers . . . Each of them was to have £100 sterling and a commission in the army if the attempt had succeeded, and that the Lord Drummond [one of the clan chiefs] was to be the governor of the Castle (38)."

Battle of Sherriffmuir

Mar, meanwhile, had raised his standard on behalf of James III on 6th September. But many believed that the cause had already come to an end as five days previously Louis XIV had died. "He was the best friend the Chevalier ever had," said Lord Bolingbroke. Even so, Mar and his forces pressed ahead and were able to occupy Perth towards the end of the month. Thereafter followed many skirmishes, but the major confrontation took place at Sherriffmuir, a stretch of moorland some two and a half miles from Dunblane in Perthshire, on 13th November, 1715. Mar had 8,000 to 9,000 men under his command, while his opponent, the Duke of Argyll, had some 3,500.

As to the battle itself, both sides considered they had won. Scott tells how "the Duke of Argyle, having returned from the pursuit of the enemy's left wing, came in contact with their

Edinburgh was dominated by the Castle, high on a crag above the town. Most of Scotland's ammunition was stored there

Government forces marching to Perth during the 1715 Jacobite
Rebellion

right . . . Mutual menaces of attack took place, but the combat
was renewed on neither side. Both armies showed a disposition
to retreat, and Mar, abandoning a part of his artillery, drew
back to Auchterarder and from thence retired to Perth. Both
generals claimed the victory. But as Mar abandoned from that
day all thoughts of a movement to the westward, his object
must be considered as having been completely defeated (39)."

The indecisive outcome of the Battle of Sherriffmuir was the
subject of a popular rhyme written just after the event by an
unknown author. It goes:

> *There's some say we wan*
> *Some say that they wan,*
> *Some say that nane wan at a', man*

Highland supporters of James, the Old Pretender, retreating from
Perth, 1716

But one thing I'm sure
That at Sherriffmuir
A battle was there which I saw, man,
And we ran and they ran, and they ran and we ran,
And we ran and they ran awa', man.

On 22nd December, James at last set foot on Scottish soil. He
had faced many dangers during his voyage from France, having
come in a tiny fishing bark to escape the attentions of the watch-
ful English navy. On 9th January, he reached Perth, but quickly
realized that his quest was at an end. Sherriffmuir had been
indecisive, it was true, but meanwhile a Jacobite detachment at
Preston had been trapped and forced to surrender.

James arrives
in Scotland

53

Meanwhile, at Perth, both sides were disillusioned by what they saw: "Instead of the hero-king of their imagination," Hume-Brown wrote, "the Highlanders saw an unimpassioned and stately person well fitted to play a part in a Court ceremony, but neither by his physical nor his mental qualities capable of inspiring enthusiasm or leading a desperate cause. . .

"Nor was the disenchantment of the Prince less grievous than their own. He had expected to find an imposing host which only required his presence to lead it to certain victory: what he saw was a motley band of 4,000 foot and 500 horse, whose sorry army presented a strange contrast to that of the disciplined troops of France in whose ranks he had served as a volunteer (40)."

Both sides might have had more respect and affection for each other had James arrived three months earlier. But as it was, after some desperate rearguard skirmishing, the Highland host dispersed among the mountains. James himself sailed back to France from Montrose on 4th February, 1715, taking with him the Earl of Mar, Lord Drummond and one or two others on whom Argyll would have loved to lay his hands.

The next attempt to put the Stuarts on the British throne by force came three and a half years after Sherriffmuir. Compared with the events of 1715, and later of 1745, the 1719 uprising was an insignificant episode, confined to one skirmish in a remote part of the Highlands. Scott called it "the last faint sparkle of the Great Rebellion of 1715." Once more however – but for the incredible bad luck of the Stuarts – the 1719 affair could well have shaken the world.

Early in 1718, not a single nation seemed likely to take up arms on behalf of the Stuarts, but by the end of the year a development in Europe filled the Chevalier's friends and supporters with the highest hopes. This time the land of promise was not Catholic France, but Catholic Spain.

The fortunes of Spain lay in the hands of a Cardinal Alberoni, the son of an Italian gardener. Alberoni had become a dominating figure on the European political scene, but a major obstacle to his ambitions was England. He therefore made up his mind to exploit the Jacobite cause for his own purposes.

Alberoni's ideas were strengthened when he heard that one *Charles XII* of the greatest warrior Kings in all history, Charles XII of *of Sweden* Sweden, was seeking vengeance against England. He felt reasonably sure he could rely on the Swedish King's active support for any plan he wished to undertake. The quarrel between George I and Charles XII had begun in the summer of 1715 when George had bought the Baltic towns of Verden and Bremen from Frederick IV of Denmark – towns that had originally belonged to Sweden and were snatched away by the Danes. Hume-Brown points out: "The rising of Mar in the autumn of 1715 offered Charles a speedy opportunity of seeking his revenge. And but for the overthrow of the Swedish fleet at Rügen, in the month of September, he would in all probability have carried out his intention of invading England. Now, therefore, he lent a ready ear to the overtures of Alberoni, and concluded a formal alliance with Spain against Great Britain (41)."

The plan was for Charles XII himself to land in Scotland at *A Swedish* the head of 10,000 Swedish troops. Such an army by itself *expedition?* would have been formidable enough, but together with the support of the clans, it could prove irresistible. Sir Walter Scott observed, however: "It might be amusing to consider the probable consequences which might have arisen from the iron-headed Swede placing himself at the head of an army of Highland enthusiasts with courage as romantic as his own. In following the speculation, it might be doubted whether this leader and his troops would be more endeared to each other by a congenial audacity of mind, or alienated by Charles's habits of despotic authority (42)."

"Amusing" is hardly the word most people would have used, *English "luck"* although it certainly would have been interesting. As it was, like nearly all its dealings with the Stuarts, the incredible luck of the English Government held once more. On the 11th December, 1718, Charles XII was killed in battle at Fredericksten, leaving Alberoni to his own devices.

These devices were plentiful enough, and the preparations for *The Spanish* the invasion of England still went ahead. James, who was *invasion* summoned by Alberoni, arrived in Madrid in March, 1719. Meanwhile, the invasion force had already sailed for England.

It was led by the Duke of Ormonde – the leading exiled Jacobite – and consisted of no fewer than twenty-nine ships and 5,000 soldiers. There was also a supply of arms for 30,000 more men.

But once again Fate intervened generously on England's behalf and the Spanish force was struck by a severe gale off Cape Finisterre. The storm, which lasted for two days, scattered the invasion fleet so far and caused such damage that the expedition had to be called off.

A token expedition was arranged by Alberoni as a diversion from the main force. This reached its destination in the Scottish Highlands. It consisted of two frigates with a detachment of 300 Spanish regular soldiers. The expedition had set sail from San Sebastian on 8th March to reach the Isle of Lewis in the Hebrides in the middle of April. Here they were joined by two Jacobite stalwarts, the Earl of Seaforth and the Marquis of Tullibardine.

An indecisive battle   Led by Seaforth, the Jacobite force occupied a pass near the great valley of Glenshiel by the head of Loch Duich. There, they were met on 10th June by a Government force of 1,100 men which included members of some Whig clans of the northern Highlands, among them the Rosses and Munroes. A half-hearted battle took place in the afternoon with neither side able to force a decisive victory. Casualties were about equal but Seaforth himself was badly wounded. So on the advice of the Jacobite leaders, the 300 Spanish soldiers laid down their arms the next day, while each clansman "took the road he liked best."

James's failure   It seemed, then, after the fourth attempt to restore the Stuarts since the Glorious Revolution, that the Jacobite cause was dead and buried. Pockets of fierce allegiance to the Old Pretender could still be found up and down the country, but in general James was not very popular. Apart from his religion, which was always a source of fear and mistrust among even most Scots, James was not the kind of man to inspire great personal affection or stir the romantic imagination.

How different it was in the case of his son, Bonnie Prince Charlie.

5 Charles–the Young Chevalier

Charlie is my darling, my darling, my darling,
Charlie is my darling, the young Chevalier!

CHARLES Edward Louis Philip Sylvester Casimir Maria Stuart is best known to history and legend as Bonnie Prince Charlie. He was the elder son of James, the Old Pretender, and a Polish princess, Clementina Maria Sophia Sobieska, and drew his first breath on 31st December, 1720. He was born in Rome at the Palazzo Muti – the splendid residence Pope Clement had given his royal parents on their wedding day.

Charles spent the first fifteen years of his life at the Palazzo. *Bonnie* He was a sturdy and active boy with a lively mind and an ear *Prince Charlie* for music and languages. At the tender age of four, a doting admirer speaks of his being "a great musician who plays on his violin continually . . . No porter's child in the country had stronger legs and arms, and he makes good use of them for he is continually in motion."

Later, when Charles was only six and a half, his cousin wrote that "not only could he read fluently . . . he could ride, fire a gun and, more surprising still, take a crossbow and split a rolling ball ten times in succession. He also speaks French, English and Italian perfectly and altogether is the most ideal prince I have met in the course of my life." Charles must have been an excellent linguist, for during 1745–46 he learned enough Gaelic to hold a conversation with his Highlanders; and Gaelic is a very difficult language.

There is no doubt that, as a child, Charles was already dis-

playing the gifts of charm and personal magnetism which in the
end destroyed him. It is equally clear that he had the gift of
courage, as befitted a descendant of John Sobieski, the great
Polish King who in 1654 drove the all-conquering Turks from
the gates of Vienna.

At the age of fourteen, for example, Charles went off to the
siege of the Italian town of Gaeta during the later stages of a
war between Austria and Spain. His cousin, the Duke of Liria,
who was helping to mop up the final Austrian resistance in the
province of Naples, described the young Prince in a letter to his
brother: "He made me pass some as uneasy moments as I ever
met with from the crossest accidents of my past life. Just on his
arrival, I conducted him to the trenches, where he showed not
the least surprise about the enemy's fire, even when the balls
were hissing about his ears. . .

"In a word, this Prince discovers that 'in great princes whom
nature marks out for heroes, valour does not wait the number of
years.' I wish to God that some of the greatest sticklers in
England against the family of Stuarts had been eyewitnesses of
the Prince's resolution during the siege, and I am firmly persuaded they would soon change their way of thinking (43)."

As to other matters, despite his fluency with languages and his
musical ability, the Prince was no scholar. This was not because
he was stupid but because he was too busy with life to bother
much with books. When he was thirteen, his tutor observed
that "the Prince grows tall and strong but it is impossible to
get him to apply to any study as he ought to do, which means that
the Latin goes ill but he speaks both French and Italian easily
(44)."

Charles is so often presented in history books as a gay and
dashing young prince that we may forget how his nature was
tinged with a streak of melancholy. He probably inherited this
from his mother. Early in his life, she began to display symptoms
of religious mania and entered a convent in Rome when he was
only five. She came back home some two years later without, it
seems, having changed much.

Anyway, her husband James, wrote to a friend in Scotland:
"She leads a most singular life. She takes no manner of amuse-

Charles Edward Stuart, known to his followers as "Bonnie Prince
Charlie" and to his opponents as the Young Pretender

ment, not even taking the air, and when she is not at church or at table is locked up in her room, and sees no mortal but her maids or so. She eats no meat this Lent, but fasts to that degree that I believe no married woman that pretends to have children ever did. I am very little with her. I let her do what she will." Clementina died, a young woman, in 1735, and her early death much affected the Prince who had been devoted to his mother.

A portrait of Bonnie Prince Charlie as a young man is given by Sir Walter Scott, whose life overlapped that of the Prince by some eighteen years: "Prince Charles Edward, styling himself Prince of Wales, was a youth of tall stature and fair complexion. His features were of a noble and elevated cast, but tinged with an expression of melancholy. His manners were courteous, his temper apparently good, his courage of a nature fit for the most desperate undertakings, his strength of constitution admirable and his knowledge of manly exercises and accomplishments perfect (45)."

Charles always showed himself remarkably tolerant in matters of religion. Unlike his grandfather, James II, he was never a bigot, although he attended church regularly enough himself.

One of his human failings was that he was a very bad speller. This can be seen from the letter he wrote to his father in 1744 from Paris: "Nobody nose where I am and what is become of me; so that I am entirely burried as to the publick and cant but say that it is a very great constrent upon me for I am obliged very often not to stur out of my room for fier of some bodys noing my face (46)."

War of the Austrian Succession But now on to the events that led up to Charles's decision to go to Scotland and raise the Stuart standard. In 1740, England went to war with Spain over who should succeed to the throne of Austria. France sided with Prussia and Spain, and Britain with Austria. However, war between Britain and France was not formally declared until March, 1744. From this conflict, known as the War of the Austrian Succession, the Jacobites hoped that somehow they would have another chance of putting the Stuarts back on the British throne. Once more, this action depended on the help of France.

 Louis XV The Jacobites' hopes began to take shape when the French

A battle during the War of the Austrian Succession. The Jacobites
hoped this war would give them an opportunity to restore a Stuart
king to the throne.

King, Louis XV, grew worried at the threat of the Dutch to join
forces with Austria and England. Louis was persuaded that the
best way of protecting his army in Flanders was by a diversionary invasion of England on behalf of the Stuarts.

Meanwhile, in Rome, the Old Pretender issued a Declaration
proclaiming his son Prince Charles "Regent of Scotland."
Charles was delighted: "The issues of war are uncertain," he
announced. "But glory is assured and my chances are splendid.
What avails hope without daring? For once I shall escape from
this inglorious idleness and look fate in the face (47)." With his
intention clear, Charles left Rome secretly in January, 1744,
bound for Paris.

Further north at Dunkirk preparations were going ahead for

the invasion of England. The plan was that Field-Marshal Saxe, one of the greatest soldiers in France and a man famed for his military skill and great strength, should land a French army of 15,000 in England. A month later Prince Charles would take up quarters near Dunkirk under the alias of "Chevalier Douglas."

The intended invasion of England was no secret to the Whitehall Government. Among the many warnings it had received came the transcript of questions put to Captain Alexander Ridley, master of a Dover packet boat. This stated that "it was common talk at Calais that 15,000 men were to be embarked on board transports in order to make a descent upon some part of His Majesty's dominions. Some said the landing was to be in Kent, others in Scotland. There were several Irish officers, and others, in company with Count Saxe, among which there was a person whom the informant saw upon the Key, and who was said by the French there to be the Pretender's eldest son, and whom they call publicly the Chevalier, and seemed to pay him a great deal of respect (48)."

Security was not very strict in those days but it has been suggested that the French were not one hundred per cent serious about invading Britain. What they merely wanted to do was scare the British Government into relaxing its pressure on the main French fleet at Toulon and on the French armies in Flanders. For that reason, it is argued, they wanted Whitehall to learn all about their activities at Dunkirk.

It seems an improbable theory, for in early March a French fleet of some twenty war ships sailed from Gravelines towards Torbay. Just off the Torbay coast they were confronted by the British fleet that consisted of "twenty-one sail of the line" under Admiral Sir John Norris. Impossible as it may sound, once again a "Protestant wind" came to the aid of the defending ships, scattering and severely damaging the invasion force. Most of the French army managed to get back to France in safety, but the damage to the fleet was great enough for Louis to abandon the whole idea.

One thing the attempted invasion by France had done was to unite the people of Britain behind the Hanoverian monarch, George II, who had come to the throne in 1727. But this display

The attempted French landing at Torbay in 1744 in support of Charles
Stuart, was frustrated by a strong English force and a severe storm

of loyalty was not directed against the Stuarts so much as
against the French. Father Cordara, a Jesuit priest and adviser
to Prince Charles, explained: "A natural rivalry had always
existed between England and France, and the English were
particularly indignant at the injury she had recently done them.
Hence though from natural inclination they might favour the
Stuarts, they could not endure the thought of this family being
restored to the throne by the French. So with one accord, they
set about preparing to offer determined resistance to the attacks
of their enemies and forestall any rising at home (49)."

In any event, the crestfallen Prince Charles finally returned to
Paris where he stayed during the winter. In August, 1744,
however, he was visited by a certain John Murray of Broughton,
a former agent of his father. Murray told him an interesting
story. According to Scott, Murray said: "If [Charles] could persuade the French Government to allow him 6,000 auxiliary
troops, 10,000 stand of arms and 30,000 *louis d'or*, he might
assuredly reckon on the support of all his Scottish friends.

But if the Prince could not obtain succour to the amount specified, they could do nothing on his behalf." Scott goes on: "The answer which the Prince returned by Murray to his Scottish adherents was that he was weary and disgusted with waiting upon the timid, uncertain and faithless politics of the Court of France; and that, whether with or without their assistance or concurrence, he was determined to appear in Scotland in person, and try his fortune (50)."

Raising an expedition

Charles's determination to get to Scotland meant there was work to be done, for plans had to be laid, money raised, arms bought and ships secured. As a start, the Prince borrowed money to buy arms, and gradually built up an arsenal in Paris consisting of 1,300 rifles, 1,800 swords, twenty pieces of artillery, powder, balls and flints. In March, he sold some of the jewellery inherited through his mother's side of the family. Best of all, through a powerful friend at court, Cardinal Tencin, he managed to persuade the French Government to loan him a "man-of-war" of 60 guns called *The Elizabeth*. To this, he added a brig, *La Doutelle* and a transport vessel, the *Du Teillay*. With Charles aboard *La Doutelle* was a small band of devoted followers. They included his former tutor, Sir Thomas Sheridan, Sheridan's son, the old Marquis of Tullibardine – a veteran of the campaigns of 1715 and 1719 – Aeneas MacDonald, a Paris banker, and a Sir John MacDonald and Captain O'Sullivan. As these names show, it was a pitifully small expedition that sailed from Nantes on the morning of 5th July, 1745. But its spirits were high, and it was confident of support in Britain – particularly as George II's army had been smashed only a few weeks before at the Battle of Fontenoy in Flanders.

Disasters at sea

But no sooner had the expedition put to sea than *The Elizabeth* was locked in bloody battle with an English man-of-war, *The Lion*. The vessels separated after doing much damage to each other, but *The Elizabeth* could not go on, and Charles ordered her back to Nantes. Two days later *Du Teillay* was forced to flee under cover of a sea mist from two other British warships, but eventually, after braving many hazards, *La Doutelle* reached Eriskay.

A good omen

The story goes that, shortly before reaching land, the Marquess

Opposite A romantic view of Bonnie Prince Charlie and the owner of *La Doutelle* (the ship in the background). *La Doutelle* had brought the Prince to Scotland before the 1745 Rebellion

of Tullibardine saw a golden eagle hovering over the ship. For him, it was an omen of good fortune: "The king of birds is come to welcome Your Royal Highness to Scotland," he is reported to have said to the Prince.

Charles must have wondered what kind of land was it that awaited his royal pleasure. He knew little or nothing of Scotland, but felt that it would be very different from France or Italy. When he saw the wild, rain-swept shore of Eriskay perhaps that streak of melancholy was already at work in his heart.

But this was no time for second thoughts or forebodings of disaster. Youth and daring might win the greatest prizes, even the most important kingdom in all Europe. In the words of one of the best known Highland airs, *The Skye Boat Song*, it was a time for optimism:

> *Sing me the song of the lad who is gone,*
> *Say, could that lad be I?*
> *Merry of heart he sailed on a day*
> *Over the sea to Skye.*

6 *The Scotland of the Prince*

MUCH OF what we know about the Highlands of Bonnie Prince Charlie's time comes from two men. Each was remarkable in his own way, and took the trouble to write down his thoughts and impressions of the region. One was Duncan Forbes of Culloden, Lord President of the Court of Session. The other was an English soldier, Captain Edward Burt, who served in the Highlands during the 1730s under General Wade, Commander-in-Chief of the British forces in Scotland.

Here is Burt's view of the Highlanders: "How often have I heard them described in London as almost giants in size, and certainly there are a great many tall men of them in and about that city. The stature of the better sort is much the same with the English or Lowland Scots, but the common people are generally small. The Highland dress consists of a bonnet made of thrum [a coarse cloth] without a brim, a short coat, waistcoat, longer by five or six inches, short stockings or brogues.

"Few apart from gentlemen wear the trowze – that is, the breeches and stockings all of one piece and drawn on together; over this habit they wear a plaid, which is usually three yards long and two breadths wide, and the whole garb is made of chequered tartan or plaiding ... This, with the sword and pistol is chiefly their mode of dressing when in the Lowlands (51)."

But the more usual dress of the Highlander was something quite different and not really appreciated by Burt: "The common habit of the Highlander is far from being acceptable to the eye. With them, a small part of the plaid ... is set in folds and girt round the waist to make of it a short petticoat that reached half-way down the thigh. The rest of the plaid is brought over the shoulders and fastened in front, below the neck and often with a fork, and sometimes with a bodkin or sharpened piece of stick, so that they make pretty nearly the appearance of the poor women in London when they bring their gowns over their heads to shelter themselves from the rain. This dress is called the quelt [kilt] and for the most part they wear the petticoat so very short that in a windy day, going up a hill, or stooping, the indecency of it is plainly discovered (52)."

The clans The clan system itself, it must be stressed, was not a feudal system with servility from the lower orders. It was more a family system, though loyalty and obedience to the chief was absolute. As Burt observed: "The ordinary Highlanders esteem it the most sublime degree of virtue to love their chief and pay him a blind obedience, although it be in opposition to the Government, the laws of the kingdom or even the law of God. He is their idol; and as they profess to know no king but him . . . so they will say they ought to do what he commands (53)."

This observation is supported by Forbes: "A Highland clan," he wrote, "is a set of men all bearing the same surname and believing themselves to be related the one to the other, and to be descended from the same common stock. In each clan there are several subaltern tribes, who own their dependence on their own immediate chiefs, but all agree in owing allegiance to the Supreme Chief of the Clan or Kindred and look upon it to be their duty to support him at all adventures (54)."

The clan system might reflect a more primitive order of society, but it would be quite wrong to assume that the clans were made up of a collection of barbarians – an assumption all too common among Englishmen at the time. The Highlander was no more uncouth than his counterpart on a farm south of the border or working in a sweat shop in a town. The fact that he spoke Gaelic (which is the same as the Erse language) and wore a kilt made him *appear* different, while his fighting qualities no doubt gave him also the reputation of being a savage. But away from the field of battle, the clansmen were rarely guilty of the atrocities often committed by the trained, professional soldiers of other armies.

68

Opposite This picture by a seventeenth-century artist is said to be the earliest painting of Highland dress

Chieftains   Their chieftains, moreover, were often men of considerable culture. Most of them were fluent in both Gaelic and English, and very often French, Latin and Greek as well. Many of them had been educated at one of the Scottish universities or in Paris or Rome. French claret was one of their favourite drinks (in addition to whisky) and like many Celts they were graceful dancers and good talkers. Something of the warlike nature of the clans, however, is reflected in their habit of estimating the size of their domains by the number of men they could muster when the "fiery cross" was sent on its round. This was a blazing wooden cross borne by relays of messengers and used to summon the clansmen to battle.

New roads   Such, then, was the way of life in the Highlands when Charles landed at Eriskay. The only real change in centuries had been an efficient system of roads built under the supervision of General Wade between 1725 and 1736. In all, some 250 miles of road linking forts and other strategic points in the region were constructed, together with forty bridges of various dimensions.

Where only rough cattle tracks had existed before, there was now a network of highways sixteen feet in width. Captain Burt wrote in a lyrical way about them in one of his letters to a friend in London: "The roads on these moors are now as smooth as Constitution Hill, and I have galloped on some of them for miles together in great tranquility. This was heightened by reflection on my former fatigue when, for a great part of the way, I had been obliged to quit my horse, it being too dangerous or impracticable to ride, and even hazardous to pass on foot (55)."

These roads were to help first the Highland army of Bonnie Prince Charlie, and then the army that destroyed him.

7 *The Prince's Early Triumphs*

IT WAS raining heavily when Charles Edward Stuart was carried from *La Doutelle* to the shore of the island of Eriskay on the back of a local fisherman. The same fisherman provided him with a meal of locally caught fish, and a bed for the night. The first person of rank to meet the Prince was the head of one of the local branches of the MacDonald clan, an Alexander of Boisdale. He gave Charles a welcome that was as chilly as the weather and advised him to return home without delay.

"But I *am* come home," the Prince replied, "and I will entertain no notion of returning to France, for I am persuaded that my faithful Highlanders will stand by me." *Charles's "home"*

The Prince began his search for the Highlanders by setting sail for the Scottish mainland on 25th July. He landed at a village called Borrodale on the shores of Loch nan Uamh (Loch of the Caves) where news of his arrival quickly spread (though his identity was still supposed to be a secret).

Alexander MacDonald, a well known Gaelic poet of the time, tells of meeting the Prince in a tent where Charles had arranged to talk with some of the leading Highland chieftains: "There entered the tent," MacDonald reported, "a tall youth of most agreeable aspect in a plain black coat and plain shirt not very clean. I felt my heart swell, but he saluted none of us and we made only a bow at some distance. At the time, taking him to be a passenger or some clergyman, I presumed to speak to him with some familiarity, yet still retained some suspicion that he might be a person of some more note. . .

"He asked me if I was not cold in my Highland dress. I

Charles landing on the mainland of Scotland in the summer of 1745

answered that I was so habituated with it that I would not exchange my dress for another. At this he laughed heartily and next inquired how I lay with it at night. I explained to him that by wrapping myself in close with my plaid, I would be unprepared for any sudden defence. But that in times of danger or war we had a different method of using the plaid so that, with one spring, I could stand to my feet with drawn sword and cocked pistol in my hand.

"Then, rising swiftly from his seat, he calls for a dram, when some person whispers to me a second time to pledge the stranger but not to drink with him. By which seasonable hint I was confirmed in my suspicion who he was. Having taken a glass of wine in his hand, he drank to us all round and soon after left us (56)."

At first, the chieftains who met the Prince at Borrodale were no more enthusiastic than MacDonald of Boisdale had been at Eriskay. But the situation changed when at last Charles turned to one of the younger MacDonalds, Ranald MacDonald of Kinlochmoidart, and said:

"You at least will not forsake me!"

"I will follow you to the death," Ranald replied, "were there no other to draw a sword in your cause (57)."

Much depended on the decision of the powerful Cameron of Lochiel. This chief was one of the first men the Prince had sent for. It had been Lochiel's declared intention to advise the Young Chevalier to go back to France.

Cameron of Lochiel

"If such is your purpose," his brother Cameron of Fassiefern told him, "write to the Prince your opinion. But do not trust yourself within the fascination of his presence. I know you better than you know yourself and you will be unable to refuse your compliance (58)."

Fassiefern was all too right. Cameron of Lochiel met the Prince, stood his ground for a little time and then was won over when Charles told him: "I have come here with my mind unalterably made up, to reclaim my rights or to perish. Be the issue what will, I am determined to display my standard and take the field with such as may join it. Lochiel, whom my father esteemed the best friend of our family, may remain at home and learn his Prince's fate from the newspapers (59)."

Charles's determination

"Not so!" Lochiel replied. "If you are resolved on this rash undertaking, I will go with you, and so shall everyone over whom I have influence (60)."

This statement was more or less the signal for the fiery cross to be lit and carried through the Highlands. On 19th August, the assembled clans met in what Sir Walter Scott called the "savage and sequestered vale" of Glenfinnan. This was a narrow glen by Loch Shiel, a few miles from Fort William. The clans came from every corner of the nearby Highlands. They included the Camerons, MacDonalds of Keppoch, MacLeods, and a host of smaller but by no means lesser clans. Here, no doubt with reverence, the ageing and arthritic Marquis of Tullibardine, that staunchest of veteran Jacobites, unfurled the Prince's red, white and blue standard. The manifesto of the Old Chevalier and the commission of Regency granted to his son were then read. Charles then made a short speech full of noble and stirring phrases, and ended by vowing that he, like the clansmen, would shed the last drop of his blood in the cause. The uprising of

Meeting of the clans

It was a great moment for Jacobite Highlanders when the Marquis of
Tullibardine unfurled Prince Charles's standard on 19th August, 1745

1745 had begun.

By this time London had heard of Charles's arrival in Scotland
as well as the news of the impending uprising. The following
proclamation was issued by the Government on 1st August,
1745: "We have received information that the eldest son of the
Pretender did lately embark in France in order to land in some

part of his Majesty's kingdoms. We, being moved with just indignation at so daring an attempt . . . do hereby in his Majesty's name, command and require all his Majesty's officers civil and military, and all other of his Majesty's loving subjects, to use their utmost endeavours to seize and secure the said son of the Pretender whenever he shall land . . . in order to his being brought to justice; and to give notice thereof immediately, when he shall be seized and secured, to one of his Majesty's Principal Secretaries of State.

". . . And we do hereby further, in his Majesty's name, promise a reward of £30,000 to such person or persons who shall seize and secure the said son of the said Pretender (61)."

Charles, by way of reply, wanted at first to offer £30 for the Elector of Hanover (George II), but he was persuaded to match the offer on his own head, as the following document makes clear.

"Whereas we have seen a certain scandalous and malicious paper . . . wherein, under pretence of bringing us to justice, like our royal ancestor King Charles I of blessed memory, there is a reward of £30,000 sterling promised to those who shall deliver us into the hands of our enemies; we could not but be moved with a just indignation at so insolent an attempt. And though from our nature and principles we abhor and detest a practice so unusual among Christian princes, we cannot but, out of a just regard for the dignity of our person, promise the like reward of £30,000 sterling to him or those who shall seize and secure . . . the person of the Elector of Hanover.

"[From] Charles, Prince of Wales, Regent of the Kingdoms of Scotland, England, France and Ireland, and the dominions thereunto belonging (62)."

It is anyone's guess where the Prince would have found £30,000 in the miraculous event of the Elector of Hanover being delivered to him. Small points like this rarely matter, however, in a war of words.

The Government had published its reward notice on 1st August. But Sir John Cope, commander of its forces in Scotland, did not hear of Charles's landing until 8th August. By that time the clansmen were well on their way south, with Perth and Edinburgh their immediate objectives. At this stage, most of the Highland troops believed they were on a large-scale raid for plunder into the Lowlands – a thought which certainly did not deter them.

"The Devil's Staircase" Cope left a hundred dragoons to guard the River Forth and marched north with some 1,500 men and 1,000 stand of arms. By 25th August he and his troops had reached the Forest of Atholl, where he was told that Charles and 3,000 clansmen were marching on the Corryarrick Pass to meet him. This Pass through Perthshire had long been used by drovers to take Highland cattle to the Lowland markets. It was known as "The Devil's Staircase." It was four miles long and had seventeen sudden turnings and a deep ditch on one side. Other hazards included a steep ascent with rocks and thickets strewn everywhere. After seeing the country, Cope realized that his men would have little chance of winning on such ground, so on 27th August he abandoned all ideas of meeting the Prince and his army. Instead of going on to Fort Augustus, he turned his troops in the opposite direction and marched to Inverness, leaving the road to Perth wide open to the Prince.

"The Moorhen" Charles, meanwhile, was swelling his army on his way to Corryarrick. There were 260 men with the Stewarts of Appin, 120 with the MacDonalds of Glencoe, and 400 with the Mac-Donalds of Glengarry – not to mention small numbers from other clans. In preparation for the battle with Cope, the Prince put on a kilt, which he wore throughout the campaign. This Jacobite song, *My Bonnie Moorhen*, tells of Charlie in his kilt:

> *My bonny moorhen has feathers anew,*
> *She's a' fine colours but nane of them blue*
> *She's red and she's white, she's green and she's grey,*
> *My bonny moorhen, come hither away.*

Charles is the "moorhen," and the colours are those of the Stuart tartan in which there is no blue.

Perth The frustration that Charles felt at not being able to get to grips with Cope and his men was soon to be replaced by jubilation when he entered Perth on 4th September. Here, he and his Highland host were joined by more supporters, among them

Lord George Murray, brother of the Duke of Atholl, whom Charles made his commander in the field. Lord Murray is not to be confused with Murray of Broughton, the Jacobite agent whom the Prince had met a year before in Paris, and who was put in charge of the administration of the campaign that was to follow. The two Murrays disliked each other intensely, and it was Murray of Broughton who had the Prince's deepest confidence.

But the talents of Lord George Murray could not be over-looked. He had fought for the Old Pretender in the campaigns of 1715 and 1719. According to Scott he was "tall, hardy and robust, and had that intuitive acquaintance with the art of war which no course of tactics can teach. He was, moreover, undoubtedly brave, and in the habit of fighting sword in hand in front of the battle. He slept little, meditated much, and was the only person in the Highland army who seemed to study the movements of the campaign. He had, however, his failings, and they were chiefly those of temper and manners. He was proud of his superior talents, impatient of contradiction and haughty and blunt in expressing his opinions (63)."

Lord George Murray

This portrait is very similar to that expressed by a Jacobite officer who fought with Murray; indeed it may have been borrowed from the officer's writings. The officer claimed that Lord George Murray used to say to his troops, "I do not ask you, my lads, to go before, but merely to follow me!" Also that he was "proud, haughty, blunt and imperious (64)."

Prince Charles and his army left Perth on 11th September. Five days later they reached the outskirts of Edinburgh, the Scottish capital. Soon after their arrival, Charles summoned a deputation from the city to hear his ultimatum. A second deputation arrived from the city at two o'clock the next morning with a petition for the Prince. It asked for time to discuss the ultimatum. But the deputies had to return saying that Charles would not agree. The only difference when they returned this time was that as they neared the Netherbow Port gate on the south side of the city, Lochiel and Murray, together with nine hundred men, swept through it "with a hideous yell."

Edinburgh

Not surprisingly, the guards at the gate offered no resistance,

Charles Stuart enters Edinburgh at the head of his army

and Charles, who rode at the head of his main force, entered the chief town of Scotland the following morning to the cheers of tens of thousands lining the streets. He was master of all he surveyed with one exception: the gaunt Castle fortress towering over Edinburgh from its giant rock.

Cope's army   Meanwhile, General Sir John Cope had not been idle. At the very hour that the Old Pretender was being proclaimed King, Cope and his army were going ashore at Dunbar, a port thirty miles from Edinburgh. They had lost no time in sailing from Inverness. General Cope had a raw but well-disciplined and equipped force consisting of 2,000 infantry and two regiments of cavalry. At Dunbar, they were joined by volunteers from various Lowland families, some of whom included a few hundred men brought by the Earl of Home. In all, Cope's army numbered

The Highland   about 3,000 men.

troops   On hearing that Cope was marching to meet him, Charles exclaimed with delight, "I have flung away the scabbard. With God's assistance, I don't doubt of making you a free and happy people (65)." His army then numbered about 2,500, having been reinforced with men from the clans Grant, MacLachlan, MacKinnon and Atholl. Its equipment left much to be desired, however, as this account by John Home, a Scots clergyman of the time, makes clear: "Sir John Cope asked what sort of appearance the Highlanders made, and how they were armed. The volunteer [Home] answered that most of them seemed to be strong, active and burly men . . . Many of them were of a very ordinary size and, if clothed like Lowlanders, would appear inferior to the King's troops, but that the Highland garb favoured them much as it shewed their naked limbs which were strong and muscular; that their stern countenances and bushy uncombed hair gave them a fierce, barbarous and imposing aspect.

"As to their arms, he said that they had no cannon or artillery of any sort . . . About 1,400 or 1,500 of them were armed with firelocks and broadswords. Their firelocks were not similar or uniform, but of all sorts and sizes, muskets, fuses and fowling-pieces. Some of the rest had firelocks without swords and some of them swords without firelocks. Many of their swords were not Highland broadswords but French . . . About a hundred of them had each in his hand the staff of a pitchfork with the blade of a scythe fastened to it, somewhat like the weapon called the 'Lochaber axe' which the town-guard soldiers carry.

"But all of them," he added, "would soon be provided with firelocks, as the arms belonging to the trained bands of Edinburgh had fallen into their hands. Sir John Cope dismissed the volunteer with many compliments for bringing him such certain and accurate intelligence (66)."

The Highland troops had a terrifying reputation long before the Battle of Killiecrankie. No troops in the world, it was thought, could possibly face the clansmen in full charge. The Chevalier Johnstone, who was *aide-de-camp* to Charles in the 1745 uprising, described their tactics in his *History of the Rebellion in Scotland in 1745 and 1746*: "The clansmen," he said, "advance with great rapidity, discharge their pieces when

The Highlanders' tactics

The Battle of Prestonpans, when the Highlanders soundly defeated the Government forces under Sir John Cope

within musket-length of the enemy, and then throwing them down draw their swords and holding a dirk [dagger] in their left hand with the target [shield] they dart with fury on the enemy through the smoke of their fire.

Fierce swordsmen "When within reach of the enemy's bayonets, bending their left knee, they cover their bodies with their targets, that receive the thrusts of the bayonets, while at the same time they raise their sword arms and strike their adversary. Their attack is so terrible that the best troops in Europe would with difficulty sustain it; and if the swords of the Highlanders once come in contact with them, their defeat is inevitable (67)." Such, then, was the army that met Sir John Cope's men early in the morning of 21st September, 1745, on a stretch of ground known as Prestonpans.

Battle of Prestonpans Cope had ordered his army to take up a position facing east, so that a long wall, which was about twelve feet high, lay immediately behind them. In front, were some fields and a road

that connected the villages of Cockenzie and Tranent. To the left, the ground sloped down to the sea, while towards the south there was a deep ditch and a marsh. The one thing Cope had overlooked was the fact that for clansmen a marsh might not be much of an obstacle. And so it proved.

A local man, Robert Anderson of Whitburgh, led the Prince's army through the marsh by a secret path in the dead of night. Even as dawn lit the sky, a thick mist still hid the two armies from each other. "Like hunters in quest of their prey," the clansmen fell upon the enemy. The English were taken badly by surprise. Worst of all, the cavalry, which Cope had put on his right and left flanks, was thrown into utter confusion. Nor was escape easy because of the wall at the rear of the English army. As a result, in about fifteen minutes of bloody action, the English army was routed and in some cases cut to pieces. One or two gallant officers, although deserted by their men, distinguished themselves by brave, last-ditch resistance. The rest, however,

The English routed

81

fled with Cope to Berwick-on-Tweed.

Bloody battlefields
"The field of battle," wrote Chevalier Johnstone, "presented a spectacle of horror, being covered with hands, legs, arms and mutilated bodies, for the killed all fell by the sword. General Cope, by means of a white cockade, which he put in his hat, similar to what we wear, passed through the midst of the Highlanders without being known. The panic terror of the English surpassed all imagination. They threw down their arms that they might run with more speed, thus depriving themselves, by their fears, of the only means of arresting the vengeance of the Highlanders. . .

"I saw a young Highlander of about fourteen years of age, scarcely formed, who was presented to the Prince, as a prodigy, having killed, it was said, fourteen of the enemy. The Prince asked if this was true. 'I don't know,' replied he, 'if I killed them, but I brought fourteen soldiers to the ground with my sword' (68)."

The Prince's story
Charles's own account of the battle story is given in a letter written on 7th October to his brother in Rome. It is remarkable for its lack of excitement and its appalling spelling: "Tis impossible for me to give you a distinct gurnal of the proceydings becose of my being so hurried with business which allows me no time; but notwithstanding I cannot let slip this occasion of giving a short account of ye Batle of Gladsmuire [the Jacobite name for the Battle] fought on ye 21 of September which was one of ye most surprising action that ever was; we gained a complete victory over General Cope who commanded 3,000 fut and to Regiments of ye best Dragoons in ye island, he being advantajiously posted with also baterys of cannon and morters, wee having neither hors nor artillery with us, and being to attack them in their position, and being obliged to pas before their noses in a defile and Bog.

"Only our first line had occasion to engaje, for actually in five minutes ye field was clired of ye Enemy, all ye fut killed, wounded or taken prisoner; and of ye horse only to-hundred escaped like rabets, one by one; on our side, we only losed a hundred men between killed and wounded, and ye army afterwards had a fine plunder (69)."

8 *To England – and Back!*

FOLLOWING the victory of his clansmen at Prestonpans, there *The route to* were three courses of action open to Charles. *London*

1. He could stay in Scotland and strengthen his hold over the country, while preparing to meet any counter-attack from the south.

2. He could invade England and march via Northumberland and Newcastle to London.

3. He could invade England and march on a western route via Cumberland and Lancashire to London.

After six weeks of holding court in Edinburgh "with great splendour and magnificence," the Young Chevalier chose the third course. The decision was made on the good advice of Lord George Murray (Charles himself had originally wanted to go via Northumberland). The reason why Charles had wanted this was that he was anxious to get to grips with Marshal Wade (of road-building fame) who was waiting for him with a newly-raised force of 14,000 men – 6,000 of whom were Dutch troops, plus 4,000 cavalry.

An interesting footnote is that this produced one more verse for the National Anthem, which is never sung today. At that time, however, it was sung with great gusto and defiance every night at the Drury Lane Theatre:

> *God grant that Marshal Wade*
> *Might by Thy mighty aid,*
> *Victory bring.*
> *May he sedition hush*

Loyal Jacobites toast Charles Stuart at the court in Edinburgh

And like a torrent rush
Rebellious Scots to crush
God save the King!

Charles's
impatience

Even before the march into England, there was plenty of reason for Charles to be content with winning back Scotland. Apart from the formidable forces building up in England, the clans themselves were hesitant about marching south of the border. To them, England was a symbol of bad luck, and they were a very superstitious people. But Charles did not share these feelings. He thought of himself not only as the heir to the Scottish throne but also to the thrones of England and Ireland. And so, after six weeks of wasted time, the march into England began on 3rd November, 1745: "As had been arranged, with the object of misleading Marshal Wade, Charles and Lord George Murray at the head of the clans proceeded by way of Lauder, Kelso, Jedburgh and Langton, while the rest of the army under the command of the Dukes of Perth and Atholl followed the western route through Peebles, Moffat and Lockerbie.

"On 9th November, Charles encamped two miles west of Carlisle, and within two hours he was joined by the detachment under Atholl. The Prince was now on English ground, and his great desire was accomplished; but the invasion had been taken against the general conviction of officers and men, and the experiences on the march had given sufficient evidence of the fact. At Kelso it was with difficulty that many of the men could be persuaded to continue in the ranks, and a full thousand had deserted before the English border was reached. A gloomy omen had further damped the spirit of the clans: as Lochiel crossed the border, he cut his hand while in the act of triumphantly unsheathing his sword (70)."

Subdued spirits

Crossing into England was a symbolic and dangerous act for the Highlanders. John Murray of Broughton observed: "It was a remarkable thing that this, being the first time they had entered England, the Highlanders, without any orders given, all drew their swords with one consent upon entering the River Tweed, and every man as he landed on t'other side wheel'd about to the left and faced Scotland again (71)."

Over the border

After some resistance, Carlisle fell to Charles and his men on 17th November. The Prince acknowledged his triumph by riding into the town on a white stallion with a procession of a hundred pipers in attendance. The next step was to continue on towards London with all possible speed. Many of the Prince's army were still reluctant to go any farther south, but Charles was impatient to get going as he felt sure that many recruits would join him in Preston and Manchester – towns where large numbers of Jacobite sympathizers were known to live.

Fall of Carlisle

As it happened, only three recruits joined the Highland Army at Preston, and two of them were Welsh. At Manchester the Jacobite High Command had been hoping for 1,500 recruits, but only two hundred "common fellows" could be persuaded to join the ranks.

Few recruits

On 1st December, Charles and his army left Manchester. They travelled through Stockport, Macclesfield, Ashbourne and Leek until on 5th December Derby was reached. This was to be a major turning point.

Back in Edinburgh, in the absence of the Highland army,

The vanguard of Charles's forces reached Manchester in November

fresh Government troops from England had reinforced the
castle garrison. Seizing their chance, castle soldiers had come to
the town on the pretence of searching for arms, but in reality
they were bent on damage and plunder. According to one
writer they "destroyed the apartment the Prince was in, tore
down the silk bed he lay in, broke and carried off all the fine,
gilded glasses, cabinets and everything else. They have done the
same to the Duke of Perth's lodging, it's entirely ruined. They
have visited the Lady Lochiel and used her in the rudest manner
calling her a bitch and whore, and had the impudence to spit in
her face . . .

"They also went to the infirmary and beat the poor Highlanders, twist about their arms and legs that was set after being
broke at the late battle, tore open their wounds so that their
shrieks were heard never so far (72)."

The Prince heard of all this, and was sympathetic, but nothing
would change his mind about going on to London. On the way
to Derby, he learned that the Duke of Cumberland, the twenty-
four year old son of George II, was in the vicinity with a Govern-

ment army of 2,200 horsemen and 8,250 foot soldiers. Cumberland who was "obscenely fat," had the reputation of being an able and ruthless officer. He was also a strict disciplinarian who would have a soldier flogged to within an inch of his life for some trifling offence.

Lord George Murray, however, had tricked Cumberland into thinking that Charles and his army were bound for Wales. As a result the Duke moved his forces to Stone leaving the way open to Derby. One can only marvel at Charles's audacity in seeking to invade London while two hostile armies were hunting him – Wade's at Newcastle, which was nearly four times as strong, and Cumberland's only a few miles away and nearly twice as strong.

Yet, nearly 150 miles away in London, there was panic. A *London in* rabble army of 70,000 men, which was reinforced with all *panic* manner of rogues and vagabonds, began to assemble near Finsbury. The few people with any money deposited in the banks withdrew it, and the royal yacht prepared to carry George II and his family away from their troubled kingdom.

William, Duke of Cumberland, led one of the Government armies against Prince Charles

The artist William Hogarth's view of the rabble Government army
that assembled in London as Charles's forces marched southward

There are many stories of how people responded to the presence of the clansmen in Derby. One is told by the well known Scottish historian and novelist of the time, Tobias Smollett, in his *History of England*: "Some Romish priests were apprehended. The militia of London and Middlesex were kept in readiness to march. Double watches were posted at the city gates and signals of alarm appeared . . . Even the managers of the theatres offered to raise a body of their dependants to serve the Government.

"The trading part of the city and those concerned in the money corporations were, nevertheless, overwhelmed with fear and dejection . . . and their countenances exhibited the plainest marks of horror and despair. On the other hand, the Jacobites were elevated to an insolence of hope, which they were at no pains to conceal, while many people who had no private property to lose, and thought no change could be for the worse, waited the issue of the crisis with the most calm indifference (73)."

Rumours of savagery As for the Highland troops stationed in Derby, their arrival was preceded by wild rumours about the savagery of the clansmen. Here is one account from the *Memoirs of the Rebellion* by Chevalier Johnstone who was at Derby with the Prince and his army: "The terror of the English was truly inconceivable, and in many cases they seemed quite bereft of their senses. One evening as Lochiel entered the lodgings assigned to him, his landlady, an old woman, threw herself at his feet. With uplifted hands and tears in her eyes she supplicated him to take her life but to spare her two little children. He asked her if she was in her senses and told her to explain herself. When she answered that everybody said the Highlanders ate children and made them their common food, Mr. Cameron assured her that they would not injure her or her little children or any other person whatever. She looked at him for some moments with an air of surprise, calling out with a loud voice, 'Come out, children, the gentleman will not eat you.'

"The children immediately left the press [cupboard] where she had concealed them, and threw themselves at his feet. They also affirmed in the newspapers of London that we had dogs in our army trained to fight, and that we were indebted for our victory at Gladsmuir to these dogs who darted with fury on the

The Highlanders' retreat north from Derby. It was the beginning of the end for the Jacobite cause

English army. They represented the Highlanders as monsters with claws instead of hands (74)."

Panic may have filled England, but Charles's chiefs were still worried by the facts. The Government had two large armies under Marshal Wade and the Duke of Cumberland, and there had still been no Jacobite uprising in England, or diversionary invasion by France.

Charles was therefore alone in thinking that London would open its gates to receive him, whatever the calibre of the "army" waiting at nearby Finsbury. So when Lord George Murray and the other chiefs of his war council informed him on the evening of their arrival at Derby, that they must go back to Scotland, the Prince reluctantly agreed.

Retreat to Scotland

The retreat began early the following morning on 6th December, or "Black Friday," as it is known in Jacobite records. There was hardly a man in the dispirited host who did not feel in his bones that this was the beginning of the end. Most of the Highland army, except the rearguard, had successfully retreated by the time Cumberland's advance force reached Clifton in Northumberland on 17th December. But the Government troops got so much the worse of the fight with the rearguard that Cumberland gave up trying to pursue the returning Highlanders.

91

Perhaps it was this victory that persuaded Charles to put a
garrison of 400 men in Carlisle Castle when he reached the
town on 19th December. Or perhaps he thought this gesture
would be a symbol of his intention to return. But for the unlucky
400 men of the Jacobite Manchester Regiment, it meant certain
capture, torture and death, and well they knew it. This is just
what they faced when the Regiment was made to surrender by
Cumberland on 30th December.

When the main body of the Jacobite army reached Glasgow
on Christmas Day, it received a chilly welcome from this normally
hospitable city. For Glasgow had been forced to contribute
money and supplies worth £10,000 to the Prince's unlucky
campaign. Charles, as one eyewitness noted, was behaving "as
if he hath a melancholy foreboding of coming disaster."

Yet before the Jacobites could be beaten, they were to gain
one more victory in the field of battle. This was on 17th January
at Falkirk, a town lying midway between Glasgow and Edinburgh. The confrontation came from an attempt by a British
army to relieve Stirling Castle after Stirling itself had opened its
gates to Charles and his forces on 4th January. In charge of the
English army, whose forces amounted to some 8,000 men,
including a strong band of cavalry, was General Henry Hawley.
Hawley had led a dragoon regiment in 1715 at Sherriffmuir and
was nicknamed "the Hangman" on account of his brutal
discipline. He was also considered a stupid man who had
learned little from his experience of war. He boasted that the
Highlanders would never stand up to a cavalry charge.

Hawley opened the battle, which took place on the Moor of
Falkirk, by sending in his 750-strong cavalry to attack the
Highland right wing under Lord George Murray. The Highlanders waited until they could see the whites of the horses' eyes,
and then fired their muskets and pistols, creating confusion and
heavy casualties among Hawley's crack dragoons. Despite
Murray's calls to gather and give help elsewhere in the battle,
the Highlanders on the right made the fatal mistake of pursuing
the flying enemy.

Chevalier Johnstone describes this section of the battle in
vivid detail: "The cavalry closing their ranks, which were

opened by our discharge, put spurs to their horses and rushed upon the Highlanders at a hard trot, breaking their ranks, throwing down everything before them, and trampling the Highlanders under the feet of their horses. The most singular and extraordinary combat immediately followed. The Highlanders, stretched on the ground, thrust their dirks into the bellies of the horses. Some seized the riders by their clothes, dragged them down, and stabbed them with their dirks. Several again used their pistols, but few of them had sufficient space to handle their swords (75)."

Meanwhile, the Highland army on the left had charged and partly broken the English right wing. But three regiments of the Government forces still stood firm. The Highlanders on this part of the field wavered, then turned back, thus communicating their uncertainty to the troops in the rear. At the same time there arose the extraordinary situation in which the left wing of each army was in headlong flight. The situation was described by the Scots clergyman, John Home, who fought at Falkirk on Hawley's side: "The battle was now in a singular state. Both armies were in flight at the same time. Hawley's cavalry and most of his infantry had been completely thrown into confusion and routed, but the three regiments on the extreme right which continued fighting had a decided advantage over the Prince's left, and many Highlanders fled under the impression that the day was lost (76)."

Confusion and flight

There were echoes of the Battle of Sherriffmuir, but as Scott points out, "The advantage upon the whole was undeniably with Charles Edward (77)." General Hawley and most of his army had fled in panic and confusion first to Linlithgow and then to Edinburgh, where on 31st January he was replaced by Cumberland as Commander-in-Chief of the Government forces.

It was Prince Charles, however, who made the worst blunder of all after the Battle of Falkirk. He went on with the siege of Stirling Castle, an activity that was quite alien to the Highland method of fighting, and in the latter half of January nearly half his army deserted him. Some were genuinely sick, others had not seen their families for six months, and others hated the prospect of spending a freezing Scottish winter taking one

Siege of Stirling Castle

Two leaders of the Jacobite garrison of Carlisle Castle led out to their
execution after the garrison's surrender to Government forces

Highland fort after another. They had fought well and faithfully
for the Prince. Now they wanted to rest and recover.

If Charles had taken the advice of his chiefs he would have
let his army rest up for the winter. Instead he exclaimed, "Good
God, have I lived to see this?" Then he "struck his head against
the wall till he staggered."

Jacobite raids As a result, ten weeks were wasted in taking large and small
forts north of the Highland line. Some people said that these
raids gave fresh spirit to the clansmen and kept the Prince's
cause alive. But that is more than doubtful. As well as exhausting
his troops, they lessened his numbers, which were already
dangerously thinned by desertions.

Eve of battle So, on the eve of 15th April, Charles and his weary, disillusioned troops found themselves in Nairn, a small town by
the Moray Firth in north-east Scotland. Murray of Broughton
had fallen seriously ill, and his troops were restless as they had
received no pay for a month. The food was so short that each
man had only one biscuit before the day of the battle. Apart
from these difficulties, the Prince had to choose whether to
meet Cumberland in open battle, or retreat into the mountains
and harass the enemy with guerilla warfare. He chose the first
option. The battle was to take place on 16th April, 1746, on
Culloden Moor.

9 Culloden – the Stricken Field

Mony's the man fought on that day
Weel the claymore could wield,
When the night came, silently lay
Dead on Culloden's field.

EVEN on the best and brightest days, Culloden Moor seems to weep for its dead. It is not just the burial stones, whose simple message tells a story more heroic than the most flowery inscription: "Clans McGillivray, MacLean, MacLachlan, Atholl, Highlanders," "Clan Stewart of Appin," "Clan Cameron," "Clan Mackintosh." On one part of the moor the grass is a little soggier, for it is near a hollow in which flows a small burn, or stream. It is nourished by a nearby spring over which is a stone bearing the words, "The Well of the Dead." To this spot crawled many wounded clansmen to slake their thirst, among them a chieftain who was shot as he was lifting his head to drink. After the battle, the pool was thick with corpses. To this day no one will drink from it.

Culloden Moor

For military purposes Culloden was a gift to Cumberland, and in particular to his chief of artillery, Colonel William Bedford. Lying some five miles to the south-east of Inverness, Culloden (or Drummossie) Moor forms part of a broad platform to the west of the River Nairn. Today, it belongs to the National Trust for Scotland, and its bleakness is obscured by a plantation of trees.

At the time of the battle it was mostly bare moorland, marshy

A Highland burial stone at Culloden. The clans buried the Highlanders where they fell

in a few places, and cultivated in small patches here and there. If Cumberland had searched the entire Highlands for a spot where his cannon could wreak the utmost havoc, he could not have found a better place. The Jacobite commander, Lord George Murray, had in fact chosen a much more suitable position a few miles away near Dalcross Castle. But Charles preferred to listen to the advice of one of his Irish officers, Captain O'Sullivan, who had personally reconnoitred Drummossie Moor and declared it "a fair field."

The wrong decision had been taken – to fight Cumberland there and then – and the wrong battlefield had been chosen. To these two grave strategic errors must now be added a list of woes and misfortunes.

First, ever since the march into England, there had been constant bickering and quarrelling between the Irish troops in the Jacobite army and the Highland chieftains. When Murray of Broughton fell ill shortly before Culloden, the influence of the Irish officers grew. Briefly, the Irish – dismissed by the clan chiefs as adventurers – were all for fighting Cumberland in open battle as quickly as possible. Win or lose, they wanted the matter settled.

The Highland chiefs, although of the same Celtic blood, were far more cautious and realistic. They did not fear Cumberland, but they knew the wretched condition of their clansmen. Lord George Murray himself believed that the Irish units "dreaded a summer campaign in the mountains."

On the side of the chiefs was the Marquis d'Eguilles, a French adviser and observer with Prince Charles's army. On the very morning of Culloden, he wrote to the French King, "In vain, I represented to the Prince that he was still without half his army; that the greater part of those who had returned had no longer their targets; that they were all worn out with fatigue, and that for two days many of them had not eaten at all (78)."

Half an army

If all Charles's men could have been mustered, some 9,000 troops could have taken the field – the same number as in the well drilled ranks of Cumberland. But, because of the mass desertions, only about half that number joined the battle on Culloden Moor.

Added to all this, most of the Prince's finest men were utterly exhausted by an exploit the night before the battle. The plan was to attack Cumberland's army at dead of night when the Hanoverian army would be off guard. This was considered an especially good night as 15th April was Cumberland's birthday and he was known not to be stingy with the brandy issue to the troops.

Exhausted soldiers

It was a daring plan which created a good deal of opposition in the Jacobite war council. But the persuasiveness of Lord George Murray and the impetuosity of Charles carried the meeting. At eight o'clock in the evening, therefore, as soon as it was dark enough to conceal the troops' movements, the twelve-mile march to Cumberland's camp began. After tramping nine miles, however, the tired and hungry force realized they would not be able to reach the enemy lines before daybreak. So, more dead than alive, the expedition returned to Culloden Moor where they immediately threw themselves down on the ground and fell into an exhausted sleep. Was it Murray or the Prince who gave the order to retreat from the night march? – this is still a matter of dispute. But Chevalier Johnstone categorically states in his *Memoirs* that it was the Prince himself who gave the order to retreat: "Had Prince Charlie slept during the whole of the expedition," Johnstone claimed, "and allowed Lord George Murray to act for him according to his own judgement, there is every reason for supposing he would have found the crown of Great Britain on his head when he awoke (79)."

Battle of Culloden

But the only crown awaiting the Prince when the two armies prepared for battle later on the morning of the 16th was a crown of thorns – or perhaps "of broken thistles." The Highland army was drawn up in two lines with the clans in the front. The MacDonalds, who had by tradition always formed the right wing of the Stuart army, were now placed on the left; the Atholl Highlanders were on the right. This was insisted on by Lord George Murray, to refute charges that he had always tried to shield his own Atholl Highlanders in battle. According to Sir Walter Scott it "seemed as if the Highlanders lost all sense of fatigue at the sight of the enemy," but that "the MacDonalds alone had a sullen and discontented look, arising from their having taken offence at the post which had been assigned them (80)."

The Government formation facing the clansmen also consisted of two lines of foot soldiers. They were widely spaced, and had a strong reserve in the rear and cavalry on each wing. There were also two guns placed between each pair of battalions in the forward line. Altogether, Cumberland had fifteen battalions of foot soldiers, seven in the front and eight in the rear amounting in all to some 8,100 men. They included a number of Lowland Scots soldiers, among them 500 Scots Fusiliers and one or two "loyal" clans such as 600 Campbells and the Monroes.

The action began about one o'clock in the afternoon with an artillery exchange that badly mauled the clans on the right wing of the Jacobite army – namely Clans Fraser, Stewarts of Appin, Camerons and Atholl. For an hour or so, these clans together with the clans of Chattan, of whom Mackintosh is the best known name, managed to keep from charging at the enemy.

The clans attack

At length the clans became so impatient they could wait no longer and so "from the centre and right wing rushed without orders furiously down, after their usual manner of attacking sword in hand . . . Notwithstanding this disorder, plus heavy losses from the cannon and grapeshot of Cumberland's artillery, the fury of their charge broke through Monroe's and Burrel's regiments, which formed the left of the Duke of Cumberland's line. But the General had anticipated the possibility of such an event, and had strengthened his second line, so as to form a steady support in case any part of his first should give way (81)."

The Highlanders charged with unabated fury towards Sempill's regiment in the second line of Cumberland's army. Here they "were within one yard of the bayonet point, when Sempill's battalion poured in their fire with so much accuracy that it brought down a great many of the assailants and forced the rest to turn back. A few pressed on but, unable to break through, were bayoneted by the first rank of Sempill's regiment (82)."

At this point the issue still hung in the balance, and there is no saying what would have happened if the MacDonalds on the left, still smarting under the imagined "insult" of their position, had fought with their usual ferocity. Instead they were hesitant and half-hearted, and it was in vain that the Duke of Perth tried to urge them on: "Claymore! Claymore!" he shouted, trying to rally them. "Convert the left into the right. Behave with your usual valour, and henceforth my name is MacDonald! (83)" *The half-hearted MacDonalds*

But only the gallant chief, MacDonald of Keppoch, and a few of his closest friends and family responded: "My God!" exclaimed Keppoch, "Have the children of my tribe forsaken me?"

To all intents and purposes, the MacDonalds *had* forsaken their chief, although with the help of some French soldiers they retreated in good order. By then, however, the battle had been lost, and the bitterest pill of all was that the finishing stroke was delivered by the "traitor" Campbell clan. *The "traitor" Campbells*

The Campbells' contribution to Cumberland's victory at Culloden was in fact more vital than spectacular. They succeeded in breaking down the walls of an enclosure on the right of Charles's army, leaving a path free for the Duke's dragoons to threaten the rear and flank of the Highland forces.

Flight was now the only course open to the clansmen if they valued their lives. Flee they did, with one troop making for the cover of the surrounding glens and mountains, their ranks *Flight*

99

Overleaf Panoramic view of the Battle of Culloden. In the foreground, messengers bring news of the battle's progress to the Duke of Cumberland

unbroken and bagpipes blaring defiance. The other limb of the Jacobite army was not so lucky. It was pursued all the way to Inverness by Cumberland's dragoons who slaughtered the armed and unarmed alike.

Cruelty and torture Chevalier Johnstone describes their behaviour: "The road from Culloden to Inverness was everywhere strewed with dead bodies. The Duke of Cumberland had the cruelty to allow our wounded to remain amongst the dead on the field of battle, stripped of their clothes, from Wednesday, the day of our unfortunate engagement, till three o'clock in the afternoon of Friday, when he sent detachments to kill all those who were still in life; and a great many who had resisted the effects of the continual rains were then despatched.

"He ordered a barn which contained many of the wounded Highlanders to be set on fire; and having stationed soldiers round it, they with fixed bayonets drove back the unfortunate men who attempted to save themselves into the flames burning them alive in this horrible manner as if they had not been fellow-creatures (84)."

That last phrase is probably the key to the cold-blooded, sadistic butchery by Cumberland's army following the battle. To many of them, the Highlanders were not fellow-creatures; they too thought of the clansmen as monsters with claws for hands, who ate children, and had man-killing dogs to fight beside them in battle.

Major James Wolfe Yet there were many honourable officers and men in the Government army who refused to join in the slaughter of the fallen. One of these was reputedly Major (later General) James Wolfe, who led the British army that stormed the Heights of Abraham during the struggle with the French for Quebec. At Culloden, the story goes, Wolfe was ordered by "Hangman" Hawley to shoot a young Jacobite commander, Charles Fraser of Inverallochie, who lay wounded on the battlefield. Wolfe refused, offering Hawley his commission instead. Not the least diverted from his purpose, Hawley found a soldier who shot Fraser in cold blood.

Casualties at Culloden In terms of casualties, Cumberland is thought to have lost about 300 men killed and wounded on Culloden Moor. This

The cold-blooded killings permitted by Cumberland after the Battle of
Culloden earned him the nickname "Butcher"

compares starkly with the Highland losses, whose dead alone
are put at between 1,000 and 1,200. A further 3,400 men were
taken prisoner before and after the battle, and many of them
either hanged, deported, or slain unarmed in the name of putting
down insurrection. How many wounded were shot or bayoneted
where they lay will never be known.

The evidence as to where Charles was during the battle is
conflicting. Some say that, on the advice of his most devoted
chiefs, he retired to a spot about a mile away from the field.
Others, such as John Home, in an extract from his *History of
the Rebellion of 1745*, believed he was on the field: "Colonel
Bedford observing the body of a horse with Charles, ordered
two pieces of cannon to be pointed at them; several discharges
were made; and some balls broke ground among the horses'
legs. Charles had his face bespattered with mud, and one of his
servants, who stood behind the squadron with a led horse in his
hand, was killed (85)."

Before Culloden, the Prince had vowed many times that he *Charles*
would conquer or die among the brave men who had risked their *escapes*
lives in his cause. When it came to the test, however, it is likely
he lost courage. "I should have died with my men at Culloden,"
he often said in later life. In any case, with the help of his
devoted clansmen he made his escape. He may not have won a
crown, but without realizing it he had won something more
precious.

103

10 Aftermath

Burnt are our homes, exiled our chiefs
Scattered the loyal men,
Yet ere the sword shall sleep in its sheath
Charlie will come again –
Skye Boat Song

BONNIE PRINCE CHARLIE never did come again to Scotland after his shattering defeat at Culloden. But the first lines of this verse were all too true. On that fateful day, the 16th April, the victorious redcoats set to work destroying the clan system.

"Butcher" Cumberland extended his bloodshed to the *Slaughter* Highlands and islands. He operated from a headquarters in Fort Augustus, one of a line of forts that straddled the Highlands from west to east. His soldiers were told to show no mercy to the local inhabitants: "They shot the male inhabitants who fled at their approach. They plundered the houses of the chieftains. They burnt the cabins of the peasants. They were guilty of every kind of outrage towards women, old age and infancy. And where the soldier fell short of these extremities, it was his own mildness of temper, or that of some officer of gentler mood, which restrained the licence of his hand . . .

"When the men were slain, the houses burnt and the herds and flocks driven off, the women and children perished from famine in many instances, or followed the track of the plunderers begging for the blood and offal of their own cattle, slain for the soldiers' use (86)."

Opposite Despite the price on Charles's head, none of the Highlanders betrayed him during his last months in Scotland

Another story is so strange that it is worth recounting. A gamekeeper called MacDonald of Glengarry came home from the forest one evening to find that a party of Government troops had ruined his crops, burnt his home and raped his wife: He swore revenge, but the only clue he had to the identity of those involved was that the soldiers had been led by an English officer on a grey horse. Twice in the weeks that followed, MacDonald saw a soldier mounted on such a horse, and twice he shot the rider dead.

The first time, however, he found he had killed the groom who was in charge of the responsible officer's horse, and on the second, an officer named Captain George Munro of Culcairn, who had nothing to do with the crime. On learning of his second mistake MacDonald broke his gun and gave up any further idea of revenge. "It is not the will of Heaven," he said, "that the person who has committed this deed shall perish by my hand. I will therefore spill no more innocent blood in the attempt (87)."

Plunder   Looting was widespread among Cumberland's men but, as John Prebble points out in his *Culloden*: "Nobody has ever prevented a victorious army from looting. Licence to kill cheapens the value of life, and respect for property falls in proportion . . . The British battalions in Scotland were old soldiers. They expected Cumberland's repeated orders against free-lance looting and they did not complain overmuch when the lash fell upon those who were caught. But neither orders nor the whip stopped them from plundering.

"Every day that Cumberland spent in Scotland after Culloden his drummers were flogging men for maurauding, and although no other General ever used the whip so much on his own men he was never successful in curbing the lust of his Army. His Orders of the Day did not help the soldiers to understand. 'No Plundering on any account,' these said, 'except by order and in presence of an officer.' Plundering was not the sin, doing so without permission was the crime . . . (88)"

Loyal clansmen   Charles, meanwhile, was to be served just as well by his Highlanders in defeat as in victory. The reward of £30,000 for his capture was known in every corner of the Highlands – the

Whitehall Government banked on the poverty and despair of the clans to betray him. But of those who could have betrayed him, not one did. Some, no doubt, were afraid of what might happen to them if they claimed the reward. Most clansmen, however, regardless of rank, shielded the Prince during his last months in Scotland out of sheer loyalty and affection.

One instance of the strength this feeling commanded was reflected in the death of Roderick MacKenzie, son of an Edinburgh goldsmith and an ex-officer in the Jacobite army. MacKenzie, who was about as tall as the Prince and looked very like him, was himself a fugitive. One day, on the hills of Glenmoriston, he was attacked and mortally wounded by a party of English soldiers. "Ah, villains!" he gasped, as he lay dying. "You have slain your Prince! (89)" *MacKenzie's cunning*

This unselfish but clever statement produced the desired effect, for the soldiers immediately cut off his head and sent it to London as that of Prince Charles Edward Stuart. Everyone in official circles believed it was Bonnie Prince Charlie's head with the result that the search for him was relaxed.

The ordeals the Prince suffered during his five months on the run after Culloden were many. One example for instance concerned Flora MacDonald, whose stepfather, Hugh Mac-Donald was a Government man and the commander of a local militia branch in Skye.

Towards the end of June, 1746, seeking to escape the attentions of the redcoats, the Prince disguised himself as Flora's maid. He adopted the name "Betty Burke" and played the part of an Irish servant girl. Lady Clanranald, wife of the man who first swore to die for Charles when he arrived in Scotland, supplied him with a "flowered linen gown, light coloured quilted petti-coat, a white apron and a mantle of dun camlet." *"Betty Burke"*

In this guise, the Prince managed to give the Government soldiers the slip, although the real maid of MacDonald of Kingsburgh (who protected Charles at the time and whose son married Flora MacDonald) was more than suspicious. She spoke of the impudence of "Miss Burke" in walking and keeping company with her master, and was amazed and vexed to see how much attention her master seemed to pay to her. "See,"

107

Flora MacDonald keeping watch over Charles as he rests after the disaster at Culloden

she told Flora, "what long strides she takes, and how her coats wamble about her. I dare say she's an Irishwoman, or else a man in woman's clothes."

On the run   Dysentery, lice, insect bites and damp clothing were some of the things the Prince had to endure, as well as the constant fear of discovery. A messenger from Lochiel who saw him about this time (July, 1746) said: "He was barefooted, had an old black kilt coat on, a plaid, philabeg [short kilt skirt] and a long red beard, a gun in his hand, a pistol and dirk by his side (90)."

Seven Men of   Although Charles was spoiled in many ways, his remarkable
Glenmoriston   cheerfulness and courtesy during these desperate days was commented on by a number of people who met him. Help and rest was to come, however, from the remarkable Seven Men of Glenmoriston. This band of Highland gentlemen had fought for Charles since the beginning of the campaign and had vowed

108   themselves never to surrender. They swore this oath: "Their

backs should be to God and their faces to the Devil; that all the curses the Scriptures did pronounce might come upon them and all their posterity if they did not stand firm to the Prince in his greatest danger and need (91)."

The Seven Men, who formed a guerilla group and worked from a cave high in Glenmoriston, consisted of two MacDonalds, three Chisholms, a MacGregor and a Grant. They hunted, stole, fought, cooked and even danced and sang for the Prince during his fifteen days with them as their guest. The royal visitor slept in the cave on a bed of heather, but claimed he was "as comfortably lodged as if he had been in a royal palace (92)."

After Glenmoriston, the Prince went in search of another *Escape to* celebrated hide-out known as "the Cage." This was the head- *France* quarters of the fugitive chieftain, Cluny MacPherson, and it was situated in a cleft on the slopes of Ben Alder, a mountain near Badenoch in Inverness-shire. On arrival, the Prince met up with two of his most famous friends once more, Cameron of Lochiel and his brother, a Doctor Cameron. It was here, too, that he

Charles Stuart left Scotland in the autumn of 1746. He never returned

The execution of Lord Balmerino, a loyal supporter of Charles Stuart, on Tower Hill, August, 1746

received word on 15th September of the arrival of the two French frigates at Loch nan Uamh. Without delay the Prince left the cave together with Lochiel and a few of their closest friends to board one of the ships, and five days later he was on his way to France. Cluny MacPherson remained in Scotland to act as a Jacobite agent.

Jacobite trials   Many brave Jacobite officers and men paid with their lives for their part in helping the Prince. Their trials were held in England, as the Whitehall Government feared that Scots juries would acquit them. In the end, it was decided to "lot" the prisoners, by picking one in twenty to face the courts. The records show that 120 were hanged; a few of them were barbarously hanged, drawn and quartered. Most of them met their fate with courage and defiance. Among the leaders of the uprising who went to the scaffold was Lord Balmerino who treated his trial with contempt. On the 18th August when his trial came to an end and he was found guilty, the court officers ended the proceedings with the emphatic prayer, "God save King George!"

"God save King James!" Balmerino responded.

A few hours before he died, a visitor apologized for intruding on his thoughts. "No intrusion at all, sir," Balmerino assured him. "For I have done nothing to make my conscience uneasy. I shall die with a true heart and undaunted; for I think no man fit to live that is not fit to die. Nor am I concerned in any way at what I have done. If I had a thousand lives to lose, I would have given them for the true King (93)."

The Prince and his party landed safely at Roscoff in Britanny *Return of a* on 16th October, 1746. The French greeted him as a hero on *hero* his return to Paris. He was granted a generous pension by the French court, and commissions were found for most of the distinguished exiles who had come with him from Scotland. Lochiel and Lord Ogilvie, for instance, were made lieutenant-colonels in the French army.

The following years gradually saw the life of the Prince degenerate into one of comfortable oblivion. His dreams became exchanged for the bottle and for the affections of a succession of women, so that by middle age he was little more than a henpecked drunkard.

In Rome on 31st January, 1788, at the age of sixty-eight, *Death of* Bonnie Prince Charlie died. It was a hundred years since his *Charles* grandfather lost the English throne. Charles spent his last hours in the arms of his daughter, Charlotte, who followed him to the grave less than two years afterwards. The only hope now for the Jacobite cause lay with the Prince's brother, Henry Stuart, or Cardinal York, the last survivor in direct line from James II. But this hope ended with Henry's death in 1807.

Jacobitism in Britain persisted as a sentimental memory for *Jacobitism:* a long time. A Jacobite club in Manchester, known as "John *a memory* Shaw's Club," did not close until 1892. Right up to the accession in 1901 of King Edward VII, finger bowls were not placed on the royal dinner table because of the old tradition by which Jacobite sympathizers would either openly or secretly toast

111

THE COUNT OF ALBANY.
PRINCE CHARLES EDWARD STUART

"The King across the water." They meant of course the Old Pretender, "King James III and VIII."

Up to the time of the First World War (1914–1918) it would still have been possible for Britain to have had a Jacobite king. This was because descendants of the Stuart royal family were – and still are – very much alive through Henrietta (1644–1670). Henrietta was the daughter of Charles I, who married and had children by the Duke of Orléans. However, by 1914, this meant that the "rightful heir" to the British throne was Prince Rupprecht of Bavaria, whom the British people would have been most unlikely to accept.

Stuart descendants

Today, the Jacobites are remembered in a number of old Scottish songs, and many of us have sung the following one when someone close to us is taking his or her farewell (94):

> *Bonnie Charlie's noo awa'*
> *Safely owr the friendly main,*
> *Mony a heart will break in twa,*
> *Should he ne'er come back again*

> *Chorus*

> *Will ye no come back again?*
> *Will ye no come back again?*
> *Better lo'ed ye canna be*
> *Will ye no come back again?*

> *Ye trusted in your Hieland men*
> *They trusted you, dear Charlie,*
> *They kept your hiding in the glen,*
> *Death or exile braving*

> *Chorus*

> *English bribes were a' in vain,*
> *Tho puir and puirer we maun be,*
> *Siller canna buy the heart*
> *That beats aye for thine and thee*

But the song was composed in honour of the Prince long after he and his cause were irretrievably lost.

113

Dramatis Personae

QUEEN ANNE (1665–1714). Brought up as a strict Protestant, married Prince George of Denmark, 1683. Several children and other pregnancies, but none survived. Dull, disagreeable but determined. Ascended throne in 1702, died in August, 1714.

ARCHIBALD CAMPBELL ARGYLL, third Duke of Argyll (1682–1761). Champion of the Whigs in Scotland during Jacobite Rebellion. Commanded Hanoverian forces at Battle of Sherriffmuir, 1715. Known as "Uncrowned King of Scotland."

DUKE OF CUMBERLAND (1721–65). Commander of Government army at Culloden, where his subsequent cruelty earned him name of "Butcher." Competent soldier but merciless. Fought and lost many a battle in Europe. Military career ended in disgrace at Hanover in 1757 where he was forced to surrender to French.

SIR JOHN DALRYMPLE (1673–1747). Another leading Government supporter in Scotland, son of James Dalrymple, first Master of Stair, and perpetrator of the infamous Massacre of Glencoe.

GEORGE I (1660–1727). Elector of Hanover, came to British throne in 1714. A courageous soldier but otherwise dull and boring. Could not speak English.

GEORGE II (1683–1760). Not unlike his father, save that he spoke English a little better. A miserly man without imagination but with an amazing capacity for detail and an excellent memory.

JAMES II AND VII (1633–1701). Second son of Charles I, created Duke of York, 1643. Father of Queen Anne (by first marriage) and of James III and VIII, the Old Pretender, by second. Ascended throne, 1685, forced to abdicate in 1688. Died in France.

JAMES III AND VIII (1688–1766). The Old Pretender. Never sat on British throne, but three uprisings on his behalf, 1708, 1715 and 1719. Father of Bonnie Prince Charlie. Died in Rome, January, 1766.

CAMERON OF LOCHIEL (died 1748). Known as "the gentle Lochiel." Chief of the Cameron clan; fought at head of his men in the 1715 and 1745 rebellions; wounded at Culloden, but subsequently escaped to France. Died in exile.

FLORA MACDONALD (1722–90). The Jacobite "heroine" who helped Bonnie Prince Charlie to evade capture during his days on the run after Culloden. Subsequently married another MacDonald and emigrated to America. Returned to Scotland in 1779.

EARL OF MAR (1675–1732). Known as "Bobbing John" because of his habit of changing sides, but leader of Jacobite forces in 1715. Yet was awarded £3,500 a year pension by George I. Died in 1732 at Aix-la-Chapelle.

LORD GEORGE MURRAY (1694–1760). First Duke of Atholl and commander of Jacobite Army at Culloden. Originally a soldier under Marlborough, but fought for Jacobites in 1715 and 1719. Brave and brilliant tactician. Died in Holland.

CHARLES EDWARD STUART (1720–88). Better known as "Bonnie Prince Charlie" and, in his day, as "The Young Chevalier." Son of the Old Pretender and "hero" of the 1745 Jacobite Rebellion. Bold, handsome, imaginative but rash and often indifferent to views and feelings of others. After losing Battle of Culloden, the Prince eventually escaped to France. Thereafter, his life was a slow process of degeneration relieved only by the bottle and his dreams. Died in Rome (where he was born) in 1788.

FIELD MARSHAL GEORGE WADE (1668–1748). English general, famous for system of roads and forts he had built in Highlands during 1720s and 1730s. Had no success against Bonnie Prince Charlie, and was replaced by Cumberland.

WILLIAM OF ORANGE (1650–1702). Dutch Prince, son-in-law of James II. Became King William III of Great Britain and Ireland in 1689. Adopted as champion of the Whigs and Protestants; bitter enemy of the House of Stuart.

A Glossary of Scots and Jacobite Terms

A' All. Pronounced *awe*.

ANE One.

AULD Old.

AWA' Away.

AYE Always.

BAIRN Child.

BAULD Bold.

BONNY Handsome or pretty.

BRAES Hills or slopes.

BREEKS Trouses or breeches.

BROGUES Highland footwear. From *brogan*, the Gaelic word for shoe.

BURN Stream or brook, the same as the old English *bourne*.

CAMERONIAN A member of the regiment formed by Richard Cameron, a staunch Presbyterian, which held the Highland forces at Dunkeld, shortly after the Battle of Killiecrankie.

CANALIA Scum. Refuse thrown into a canal.

CAVALIER A mounted soldier. A name given to the gentlemen who fought for Charles I against Oliver Cromwell during the Civil War, and thereafter identified with the supporters of the Jacobite cause.

CHATEAU French for "castle," and sometimes used to mean mansions or large houses.

CHEVALIER The French word for a knight, or gallant young man. Hence, Bonnie Prince Charlie was known as "The Young Chevalier."

CLAYMORE A Highland broadsword, a weapon universally

117

feared by all who met the clansmen in battle. Literally from the Gaelic *claidh mor,* meaning a big knife.

CLEEKS Old Scottish word for "tucks in" – not of food but of clothes.

COCKADE A decoration resembling a cock's crest, worn in the hat. The Jacobite or Stuart symbol was a white cockade.

COVENANTER A supporter of the Scottish Solemn League and Covenant, a seventeenth century declaration by Scots to defend their Presbyterian religion against the Churches of Rome and England, if need be.

CUIRASS A piece of defensive armour covering the body from neck to waist.

DEIL Devil.

DIVINE RIGHT The doctrine that monarchs were appointed by God, and so were responsible to God alone.

DRAGOON A soldier who was taught and armed to serve either on horseback or foot.

DRAM A measure of drink, usually whisky.

DUDS Clothes.

DURST Dare.

EPISCOPALIAN Literally, government by bishops as in the Church of England. At the time of the Jacobite Rebellion, although there was an Episcopal Church in Scotland, most of the Scots population were Presbyterian. By contrast, most members of the Episcopal and Catholic Churches in Scotland supported the Jacobite cause.

GADE Gone, went.

GIRT Wearing a belt, to surround.

HABIT Dress.

HIELAND Scottish spelling of Highland. Sometimes written as "Hielan."

ITHER Other.

JACOBITE From *Jacobus,* Latin for James. A supporter of the claim of James II and later of his son, James, to be the true and rightful King of Great Britain and Ireland.

KAIL-YARDIE Cabbage patch.

KENT Knew.

LAIRDIE A minor Scottish noble. Diminutive form of laird.

LEVEE A royal audience.

LO'ED Loved.

MAUN Must.

NANE None.

NOO Now.

PICQUET The French form of "picket." A guard posted in front of an army to keep watch.

PLAID A tartan blanket or broadcloth. Part of the kilt.

PRESBYTERIAN One who believes that a Church should be governed by elders, as in the Church of Scotland, where, during the Jacobite Rebellions, the Presbyterians were on the side of the Government and the Hanoverian royal family.

PRINCIPALITY The territory of a prince, such as Wales.

PUIR Poor.

RAWS Raw but good fighting men.

RUDE Rough, unpolished.

SAE So.

SEPT A branch of a clan, a sub-section of the tribe.

SICCAN Such.

SILLER Silver.

SLEUGHING Peeling or stripping. Scottish equivalent of "sloughing."

STEM Used by James Hogg to describe an offspring of a family.

STRAND Beach.

TORY Originally a Gaelic word meaning a robber or pursuer, but by the time of Jacobite Rebellion it had come to denote a supporter of the conservative party in England, and they as a rule were sympathetic with the Jacobite cause.

WAN Won.

WEE Small.

WEEL Well.

WELL-AFFECTED In sympathy with.

WHIG From the Scottish word "whig," meaning "whey." The Scottish covenanters used to drink this, hence the name became associated with their religious and political beliefs.

Table of Dates

1688	June. Birth of James III and VIII, the Old Pretender. Prince William of Orange lands at Torbay on 5th November with invasion force to take over the government of Britain as King William III.
1689	James II flees in January to France. July. Battle of Killiecrankie. Bonnie Dundee wins for the Jacobites.
1690	Highland clans defeated at Cromdale, on 1st May. 12th July. King William defeats James II at Battle of the Boyne in Northern Ireland.
1692	February. Massacre of Glencoe.
1695	July. Scottish merchants launch Darien Expedition.
1700	Scots forced to abandon Darien Scheme.
1701	September. Death of James II and VII.
1702	March. Death of William III. Queen Anne succeeds to British throne.
1707	Union of the Parliaments of England and Scotland.
1708	March. French invasion fleet sails for Scotland to help establish Old Pretender on British throne. Expedition proves abortive.
1714	1st August. Death of Queen Anne. September. George I, Elector of Hanover, is proclaimed sovereign of Great Britain and Ireland.
1715	Third Jacobite Rebellion. Indecisive Battle of Sherriffmuir fought on 13th November. December. James III and VIII lands in Scotland.
1716	February. James sails for France with leading Jacobite "rebels."

1719	March. Spanish invasion fleet sails for Britain, but is scattered by bad weather.
	Fourth Jacobite uprising defeated on 10th June at Glenshiel.
1720	Birth of Charles Edward Stuart, Bonnie Prince Charlie, at Rome on 31st December.
1727	Death of George I, who is succeeded by his son, George II.
1725– 1736	General Wade builds network of 250 miles of good roads in the Highlands, and a string of forts.
1744	March. War declared between Britain and France. French invasion force sails for Britain but is turned back by storms and the British Navy.
1745	Fifth and final Jacobite attempt to restore the House of Stuart in July. Bonnie Prince Charlie lands in Scotland; clans rally to him.
	September. Bonnie Prince Charlie and the Highland army occupy Edinburgh.
	September. Highland army defeats the forces of General Sir John Cope at Prestonpans (known by Jacobites as the Battle of Gladsmuir).
	November. Highland army under Charles marches south into England, reaches Derby on 5th December. Turns back to Scotland the following day.
1746	January. Battle of Falkirk. Bonnie Prince Charlie's army wins second major victory but fails to follow it up.
	16th April. Culloden. Duke of Cumberland's army crushes the Highland clans in the decisive battle of the Jacobite Rebellion.
	Clansmen forbidden to carry arms or to wear the kilt. This ban was not lifted until 1782.
1766	Death of James III and VIII, father of Bonnie Prince Charlie.
1788	31st January. Death in Rome of Bonnie Prince Charlie himself.

List of Sources

(1) Sir Walter Scott *Tales of a Grandfather*
(2) *Ibid*
(3) *Ibid*
(4) *Ibid*
(5) *Ibid*
(6) *Ibid*
(7) *Ibid*
(8) Sir Walter Scott, *Poems*
(9) P. Hume-Brown, *History of Scotland* (Vol II)
(10) *Ibid*
(11) *Ibid*
(12) John Dryden, *Poems*
(13) James Hogg, *Relics of the Jacobite Rebellion*
(14) Sir John Dalrymple, *Letters*
(15) Sir Walter Scott, *Tales of a Grandfather*
(16) *Ibid*
(17) Sir John Dalrymple, *op. cit.*
(18) *Ibid*
(19) Order issued by Major Robert Duncanson to Captain Campbell of Glenlyon
(20) Sir Walter Scott, *Tales of a Grandfather*
(21) *Ibid*
(22) Hodge, *Vindication of the Scots Design*
(23) Speech of the Duke of Hamilton to Scots Parliament, October, 1706 Quoted from Wood's *Peerage*
(24) Sir Walter Scott, *Tales of a Grandfather*
(25) George Lockhart of Carnwath, *Papers*

(26) Sir Walter Scott, *Tales of a Grandfather*
(27) George Lockhart of Carnwath, *op. cit.*
(28) Sir Walter Scott, *Tales of a Grandfather*
(29) Correspondence of Admiral Forbin
(30) *Ibid*
(31) George Lockhart of Carnworth, *op. cit.*
(32) *Ibid*
(33) James Hogg, *op. cit.*
(34) *Ibid*
(35) P. Hume-Brown, *op. cit.*
(36) *Ibid*
(37) James Hogg, *op. cit.*
(38) James Rae, *History of the 1715 Rebellion*
(39) *Ibid*
(40) P. Hume-Brown, *op. cit.*
(41) *Ibid*
(42) Sir Walter Scott, *Tales of a Grandfather*
(43) Stuart Papers at Windsor
(44) *Ibid*
(45) Sir Walter Scott, *Tales of a Grandfather*
(46) Letters of Charles Edward Stuart
(47) *Ibid*
(48) Quoted by Moray McLaren in his biography of *Bonnie Prince Charlie*
(49) *Ibid*
(50) Sir Walter Scott, *Tales of a Grandfather*
(51) Captain Edward Burt, *Letters from the North*
(52) *Ibid*

(53) *Ibid*
(54) Duncan Forbes, *Culloden Papers*
(55) Captain Edward Burt, *Letters from the North*
(56) George Lockhart of Carnwath, *op. cit.*
(57) Sir Walter Scott, *Tales of a Grandfather*
(58) *Ibid*
(59) *Ibid*
(60) *Ibid*
(61) Proclamation of the Whitehall Government, August, 1745
(62) H. V. Morton. Quoted from his travel book, *In Search of Scotland*
(63) Sir Walter Scott, *Tales of a Grandfather*
(64) *Ibid*
(65) Sir Walter Scott, *Prose Works*
(66) John Home, *The History of the Rebellion in Scotland, 1745*
(67) Chevalier Johnstone, *Memoirs of the Rebellion in Scotland in 1745 and 1746*
(68) *Ibid*
(69) Letters of Prince Charles Edward Stuart
(70) P. Hume-Brown, *op. cit.*
(71) *Ibid*
(72) Quoted by Moray McLaren in *op. cit.*
(73) Tobias Smollett. *A Complete History of England*
(74) Chevalier Johnstone, *op. cit.*
(75) *Ibid*

(76) John Home, *op. cit.*
(77) Sir Walter Scott, *Tales of a Grandfather*
(78) Quoted by Moray McLaren in *op. cit.*
(79) Chevalier Johnstone, *op. cit.*
(80) Sir Walter Scott, *Tales of a Grandfather*
(81) *Ibid*
(82) *Ibid*
(83) *Ibid*
(84) Chevalier Johnstone, *op. cit.*
(85) John Home, *op. cit.*
(86) Sir Walter Scott, *Tales of a Grandfather*
(87) *Ibid*
(88) John Prebble, *Culloden*
(89) Chevalier Johnstone, *op. cit.*
(90) Quoted by Moray MacLaren, *op. cit.*
(91) John Prebble, *Culloden*
(92) Eric Linklater, *The Prince in the Heather*
(93) Sir Walter Scott, *Tales of a Grandfather*
(94) Baroness Nairne, Traditional Jacobite air

Picture Credits

The author and publishers wish to thank those who have given permission for copyright illustrations to appear on the pages mentioned: Trustees of the Glasgow Art Gallery, jacket; the Trustees of the British Museum, 35; the Mansell Collection, 33, 65, 69, 74, 91, 96, 100–101, 103, 109, 112; the Radio Times Hulton Picture Library, frontispiece, 8, 12–13, 14, 15, 16–17, 18, 22, 23, 25, 26, 38–39, 42, 46, 51, 52, 53, 59, 61, 63, 72, 78, 80–81, 84, 86, 87, 88–89, 94, 104, 108, 110.

Further Reading

There is no shortage of literature on the Jacobite Rebellion for students who wish to learn more of this fascinating struggle. The more important sources – contemporary and modern – are as follows: *The Memorials of John Murray of Broughton, Sometime Secretary to Prince Charles Edward 1740–1747* (The Scottish History Society, Vol XXVII, Edinburgh, 1898); *The Lyon in Mourning*. Eyewitness accounts, letters and other documents on Culloden and its aftermath, collected by the Reverend Robert Forbes, Bishop of Ross and Caithness, 1746–1775 (The Scottish History Society, Vols XX–XXII, Edinburgh, 1895); *Memoirs of the Rebellion in Scotland in 1745 and 1746*, the Chevalier de Johnstone (Folio Society, 1958); *A Short Account of the Affairs of Scotland, 1744 to 1747*, Lord Elcho (Douglas, Edinburgh, 1907); *The Rising of 1745*, C. S. Terry (Cambridge University Press, 1903); *Tales of a Grandfather*, Sir Walter Scott (Black); and *The Jacobite Relics of Scotland*, James Hogg (First published 1819–1821. Reprinted by AMS Press Inc., New York).

Various publications give the Government or Whig point of view, by men actually involved in the fighting or in the politics of the time. These include: *The Culloden Papers*, Duncan Forbes, Lord President of the Scottish Court of Sessions; *A Compleat History of the Rebellion*, James Ray, a volunteer in the Duke of Cumberland's army (First published in York, 1789); and *A History of the Rebellion in the Year 1745*,

John Home, a Scots minister taken prisoner at the Battle of Falkirk (1802).

A complementary view to *The Culloden Papers* is provided by two volumes known as *The Lockhart Papers*. These were written by George Lockhart of Carnwath, a devoted but critical supporter of James III and VIII, the Old Pretender.

Finally, any list of contemporary literature on the Rebellion must mention Bonnie Prince Charlie's own version of these events. This appears in his *Commentary on the Expedition to Scotland*, compiled by an Italian priest, Padre Giulio Cesare Cordara, in 1751 (The Scottish History Society).

More recent publications about the Jacobites include: *Culloden*, John Prebble (Secker and Warburg, 1961); *The Battles of the Forty-five*, Katherine Tomasson and Francis Buist (Batsford, 1962); *The Jacobite General*, Katherine Tomasson (Edinburgh, Blackwood, 1958); and *The Jacobite Movement: The Last Phase*, Sir Charles Petrie (Eyre and Spottiswoode, 1959).

There are numerous biographies of the Prince himself and his adventures. They include: *Prince Charles Edward*, Winifred Duke (Hale, 1938); *Death of a Legend*, Peter de Polnay (Hamish Hamilton, 1952); *The Prince in the Heather*, Eric Linklater (Hodder and Stoughton, 1965); *Bonnie Prince Charlie*, Moray McLaren (Ruper Hart-Davis, 1972); and *Prince Charlie and his Ladies*, Sir Compton Mackenzie (Dobson, 1966).

Finally, for a balanced view of the impact of the Jacobite rebellions on the development of Britain and of Scotland in particular, there is no better account than *The Mainstream of Jacobitism* by George Hilton Jones, published in 1954 by Harvard University Press. *The Stuart Papers at Windsor*, published in 1939, should also be studied by those interested in the early life of Prince Charles Edward Stuart.

Index

128